60 Donut Recipes for Home

By: Kelly Johnson

Table of Contents

- Classic Glazed Donuts
- Chocolate Glazed Donuts
- Maple Bacon Donuts
- Blueberry Cake Donuts
- Cinnamon Sugar Donuts
- Lemon Glazed Donuts
- Pumpkin Spice Donuts
- Red Velvet Donuts
- Matcha Green Tea Donuts
- Strawberry Shortcake Donuts
- Cookies and Cream Donuts
- Nutella-filled Donuts
- Raspberry Jelly-filled Donuts
- Coffee Glazed Donuts
- S'mores Donuts
- Apple Cider Donuts
- Coconut Lime Donuts
- Pistachio Glazed Donuts
- Mocha Almond Fudge Donuts
- Churro Donuts
- Chocolate Mint Donuts
- Pina Colada Donuts
- Brown Butter Bourbon Donuts
- Almond Joy Donuts
- Funfetti Donuts
- Cherry Cheesecake Donuts
- Salted Caramel Pretzel Donuts
- Double Chocolate Chunk Donuts
- Raspberry White Chocolate Donuts
- Orange Creamsicle Donuts
- Peanut Butter Cup Donuts
- Blackberry Lavender Donuts
- Blueberry Lemon Glazed Donuts
- Carrot Cake Donuts
- Dulce de Leche Donuts

- Honey Glazed Donuts
- Pistachio Cherry Donuts
- Pineapple Upside-Down Donuts
- Cranberry Orange Donuts
- White Chocolate Raspberry Donuts
- Raspberry Almond Donuts
- Irish Cream Glazed Donuts
- Banana Nut Donuts
- Chocolate Peanut Butter Pretzel Donuts
- Vanilla Bean Glazed Donuts
- Triple Chocolate Donuts
- Key Lime Pie Donuts
- Rum Raisin Donuts
- Pistachio Rosewater Donuts
- Caramel Apple Donuts
- Lavender Honey Donuts
- Pomegranate Blueberry Donuts
- Gingerbread Spiced Donuts
- Chocolate Cherry Cordial Donuts
- Coconut Mango Donuts
- Strawberry Basil Donuts
- Caramel Macchiato Donuts
- Rosemary Olive Oil Donuts
- Banana Foster Donuts
- Chocolate Hazel Crunch Donuts

Classic Glazed Donuts

Ingredients:

For the Donuts:

- 2 ¼ teaspoons (1 packet) active dry yeast
- 2 tablespoons warm water (about 110°F/43°C)
- 3/4 cup warm milk (about 110°F/43°C)
- 1/4 cup granulated sugar
- 1/4 cup unsalted butter, softened
- 1/2 teaspoon salt
- 1 large egg
- 3 cups all-purpose flour
- Vegetable oil (for frying)

For the Glaze:

- 2 cups powdered sugar
- 1/4 cup milk
- 1 teaspoon vanilla extract

Instructions:

In a small bowl, combine the active dry yeast and warm water. Let it sit for 5 minutes until it becomes foamy.
In a large mixing bowl, combine the warm milk, sugar, softened butter, salt, and egg. Add the yeast mixture and mix well.
Gradually add the flour, one cup at a time, stirring until a soft dough forms.
Turn the dough onto a floured surface and knead for about 5 minutes until it becomes smooth and elastic.
Place the dough in a greased bowl, cover it with a clean cloth, and let it rise in a warm place for 1-1.5 hours or until doubled in size.
Roll out the dough on a floured surface to about 1/2-inch thickness. Cut out donut shapes using a donut cutter or two differently sized round cookie cutters.
Heat vegetable oil in a deep fryer or large, deep saucepan to 350°F (175°C).

Carefully place the donuts into the hot oil, frying each side until golden brown (about 1-2 minutes per side).

Remove the donuts with a slotted spoon and place them on a paper towel-lined plate to absorb excess oil.

In a bowl, whisk together powdered sugar, milk, and vanilla extract to make the glaze.

Dip each donut into the glaze, ensuring they are well coated, and place them on a wire rack to set.

Allow the glaze to set for about 15 minutes, and then your Classic Glazed Donuts are ready to enjoy!

Feel free to customize the glaze or add sprinkles for an extra touch. Enjoy your delicious homemade donuts!

Chocolate Glazed Donuts

Ingredients:

For the Donuts:

- 2 ¼ teaspoons (1 packet) active dry yeast
- 2 tablespoons warm water (about 110°F/43°C)
- 3/4 cup warm milk (about 110°F/43°C)
- 1/4 cup granulated sugar
- 1/4 cup unsalted butter, softened
- 1/2 teaspoon salt
- 1 large egg
- 3 cups all-purpose flour
- Vegetable oil (for frying)

For the Chocolate Glaze:

- 1/2 cup semisweet chocolate chips
- 3 tablespoons unsalted butter
- 1 cup powdered sugar
- 1/4 cup unsweetened cocoa powder
- 1/4 cup milk
- 1 teaspoon vanilla extract
- Pinch of salt

Instructions:

In a small bowl, combine the active dry yeast and warm water. Let it sit for 5 minutes until it becomes foamy.

In a large mixing bowl, combine the warm milk, sugar, softened butter, salt, and egg. Add the yeast mixture and mix well.

Gradually add the flour, one cup at a time, stirring until a soft dough forms.

Turn the dough onto a floured surface and knead for about 5 minutes until it becomes smooth and elastic.

Place the dough in a greased bowl, cover it with a clean cloth, and let it rise in a warm place for 1-1.5 hours or until doubled in size.

Roll out the dough on a floured surface to about 1/2-inch thickness. Cut out donut shapes using a donut cutter or two differently sized round cookie cutters.

Heat vegetable oil in a deep fryer or large, deep saucepan to 350°F (175°C). Carefully place the donuts into the hot oil, frying each side until golden brown (about 1-2 minutes per side).

Remove the donuts with a slotted spoon and place them on a paper towel-lined plate to absorb excess oil.

For the chocolate glaze, melt the chocolate chips and butter in a bowl. Add powdered sugar, cocoa powder, milk, vanilla extract, and a pinch of salt. Mix until smooth.

Dip each donut into the chocolate glaze, ensuring they are well coated, and place them on a wire rack to set.

Allow the glaze to set for about 15 minutes, and then your Chocolate Glazed Donuts are ready to be enjoyed!

Feel free to add chocolate sprinkles or chopped nuts to enhance the flavor. Enjoy your homemade chocolate glazed donuts!

Maple Bacon Donuts

Ingredients:

For the Donuts:

- 2 ¼ teaspoons (1 packet) active dry yeast
- 2 tablespoons warm water (about 110°F/43°C)
- 3/4 cup warm milk (about 110°F/43°C)
- 1/4 cup granulated sugar
- 1/4 cup unsalted butter, softened
- 1/2 teaspoon salt
- 1 large egg
- 3 cups all-purpose flour
- Vegetable oil (for frying)

For the Maple Glaze:

- 1/2 cup pure maple syrup
- 1 1/2 cups powdered sugar
- 2 tablespoons unsalted butter, melted
- 1 teaspoon vanilla extract
- Pinch of salt

For the Bacon Topping:

- 6-8 slices of bacon, cooked and crumbled

Instructions:

In a small bowl, combine the active dry yeast and warm water. Let it sit for 5 minutes until it becomes foamy.
In a large mixing bowl, combine the warm milk, sugar, softened butter, salt, and egg. Add the yeast mixture and mix well.
Gradually add the flour, one cup at a time, stirring until a soft dough forms.
Turn the dough onto a floured surface and knead for about 5 minutes until it becomes smooth and elastic.
Place the dough in a greased bowl, cover it with a clean cloth, and let it rise in a warm place for 1-1.5 hours or until doubled in size.

Roll out the dough on a floured surface to about 1/2-inch thickness. Cut out donut shapes using a donut cutter or two differently sized round cookie cutters. Heat vegetable oil in a deep fryer or large, deep saucepan to 350°F (175°C). Carefully place the donuts into the hot oil, frying each side until golden brown (about 1-2 minutes per side).

Remove the donuts with a slotted spoon and place them on a paper towel-lined plate to absorb excess oil.

For the maple glaze, whisk together maple syrup, powdered sugar, melted butter, vanilla extract, and a pinch of salt until smooth.

Dip each donut into the maple glaze, ensuring they are well coated, and place them on a wire rack to set.

While the glaze is still tacky, sprinkle crumbled bacon on top of each donut. Allow the glaze to set for about 15 minutes, and then your Maple Bacon Donuts are ready to be enjoyed!

The combination of maple glaze and bacon adds a perfect balance of sweetness and savory goodness. Enjoy your homemade Maple Bacon Donuts!

Blueberry Cake Donuts

Ingredients:

For the Donuts:

- 2 cups all-purpose flour
- 1/2 cup granulated sugar
- 1 1/2 teaspoons baking powder
- 1/4 teaspoon baking soda
- 1/2 teaspoon salt
- 1/2 teaspoon ground cinnamon
- 1/2 cup buttermilk
- 2 large eggs
- 1/4 cup unsalted butter, melted
- 1 teaspoon vanilla extract
- 1 cup fresh or frozen blueberries (if using frozen, do not thaw)

For the Glaze:

- 1 cup powdered sugar
- 2 tablespoons milk
- 1/2 teaspoon vanilla extract

Instructions:

Preheat your oven to 375°F (190°C) and grease a donut pan.
In a large bowl, whisk together the flour, sugar, baking powder, baking soda, salt, and cinnamon.
In a separate bowl, whisk together the buttermilk, eggs, melted butter, and vanilla extract.
Add the wet ingredients to the dry ingredients and stir until just combined. Gently fold in the blueberries.
Spoon the batter into a piping bag or a zip-top bag with the corner snipped off.
Pipe the batter into the prepared donut pan, filling each cavity about 2/3 full.
Bake for 12-15 minutes or until the donuts are golden brown and a toothpick inserted into the center comes out clean.

Allow the donuts to cool in the pan for a few minutes before transferring them to a wire rack to cool completely.

For the glaze, whisk together powdered sugar, milk, and vanilla extract in a bowl until smooth.

Dip each cooled donut into the glaze, making sure to coat the top. Place them back on the wire rack to allow the glaze to set.

Enjoy your delicious Blueberry Cake Donuts with a cup of coffee or your favorite beverage!

Feel free to customize these donuts by adding a lemon zest to the glaze or a sprinkle of powdered sugar for an extra touch. These blueberry cake donuts are sure to be a hit!

Cinnamon Sugar Donuts

Ingredients:

For the Donuts:

- 2 cups all-purpose flour
- 1/2 cup granulated sugar
- 1 tablespoon baking powder
- 1/2 teaspoon salt
- 1/2 teaspoon ground cinnamon
- 3/4 cup buttermilk
- 2 large eggs
- 1/4 cup unsalted butter, melted
- 1 teaspoon vanilla extract

For the Cinnamon Sugar Coating:

- 1/2 cup granulated sugar
- 1 teaspoon ground cinnamon
- 1/4 cup unsalted butter, melted

Instructions:

Preheat your oven to 375°F (190°C). Grease a donut pan.
In a large bowl, whisk together the flour, sugar, baking powder, salt, and ground cinnamon.
In a separate bowl, whisk together the buttermilk, eggs, melted butter, and vanilla extract.
Add the wet ingredients to the dry ingredients and stir until just combined. Do not overmix.
Spoon the batter into a piping bag or a zip-top bag with the corner snipped off.
Pipe the batter into the prepared donut pan, filling each cavity about 2/3 full.
Bake for 12-15 minutes or until the donuts are golden brown and a toothpick inserted into the center comes out clean.
While the donuts are baking, prepare the cinnamon sugar coating. In a shallow bowl, mix together sugar and ground cinnamon.

Once the donuts are out of the oven and slightly cooled, brush each donut with melted butter and then roll it in the cinnamon sugar mixture, ensuring it's well coated.

Place the coated donuts on a wire rack to cool completely.

Enjoy your homemade Cinnamon Sugar Donuts with a cup of coffee or tea!

These donuts are wonderfully fluffy and coated in a sweet cinnamon sugar mixture, making them a delightful treat for any occasion.

Lemon Glazed Donuts

Ingredients:

For the Donuts:

- 2 cups all-purpose flour
- 1/2 cup granulated sugar
- 1 tablespoon baking powder
- 1/2 teaspoon salt
- 1/2 cup buttermilk
- 2 large eggs
- 1/4 cup unsalted butter, melted
- Zest of 2 lemons
- 2 tablespoons freshly squeezed lemon juice
- 1 teaspoon vanilla extract

For the Lemon Glaze:

- 1 1/2 cups powdered sugar
- 3 tablespoons freshly squeezed lemon juice
- Zest of 1 lemon

Instructions:

Preheat your oven to 375°F (190°C). Grease a donut pan.
In a large bowl, whisk together the flour, sugar, baking powder, and salt.
In a separate bowl, whisk together the buttermilk, eggs, melted butter, lemon zest, lemon juice, and vanilla extract.
Add the wet ingredients to the dry ingredients and stir until just combined. Do not overmix.
Spoon the batter into a piping bag or a zip-top bag with the corner snipped off.
Pipe the batter into the prepared donut pan, filling each cavity about 2/3 full.
Bake for 12-15 minutes or until the donuts are golden brown and a toothpick inserted into the center comes out clean.
While the donuts are baking, prepare the lemon glaze. In a bowl, whisk together powdered sugar, lemon juice, and lemon zest until smooth.
Once the donuts are out of the oven and slightly cooled, dip each donut into the lemon glaze, ensuring they are well coated.

Place the glazed donuts on a wire rack to allow the glaze to set.
Enjoy your zesty Lemon Glazed Donuts as a delightful treat!

The combination of the bright lemon flavor with the sweet glaze makes these donuts a perfect choice for a refreshing dessert or snack.

Pumpkin Spice Donuts

Ingredients:

For the Donuts:

- 2 cups all-purpose flour
- 1 1/2 teaspoons baking powder
- 1/2 teaspoon baking soda
- 1/2 teaspoon salt
- 1 teaspoon ground cinnamon
- 1/2 teaspoon ground nutmeg
- 1/4 teaspoon ground cloves
- 1/4 teaspoon ground ginger
- 1/2 cup unsalted butter, softened
- 1/2 cup brown sugar, packed
- 1/2 cup granulated sugar
- 2 large eggs
- 1 cup canned pumpkin puree
- 1 teaspoon vanilla extract
- 1/2 cup buttermilk

For the Cinnamon Sugar Coating:

- 1/2 cup granulated sugar
- 1 teaspoon ground cinnamon
- 1/4 cup unsalted butter, melted

Instructions:

Preheat your oven to 350°F (175°C). Grease a donut pan.
In a medium bowl, whisk together the flour, baking powder, baking soda, salt, cinnamon, nutmeg, cloves, and ginger.
In a large bowl, cream together the softened butter, brown sugar, and granulated sugar until light and fluffy.
Add the eggs one at a time, beating well after each addition. Then, mix in the pumpkin puree and vanilla extract.

Gradually add the dry ingredients to the wet ingredients, alternating with buttermilk, beginning and ending with the dry ingredients. Mix until just combined.

Spoon the batter into a piping bag or a zip-top bag with the corner snipped off. Pipe the batter into the prepared donut pan, filling each cavity about 2/3 full.

Bake for 12-15 minutes or until the donuts are firm and a toothpick inserted into the center comes out clean.

While the donuts are baking, prepare the cinnamon sugar coating. In a shallow bowl, mix together sugar and ground cinnamon.

Once the donuts are out of the oven and slightly cooled, brush each donut with melted butter and then roll it in the cinnamon sugar mixture, ensuring it's well coated.

Place the coated donuts on a wire rack to cool completely.

Enjoy your Pumpkin Spice Donuts with a sprinkle of fall goodness!

These pumpkin spice donuts are sure to be a hit with their warm and comforting flavors. Perfect for cozy autumn mornings or as a treat for any pumpkin lover!

Red Velvet Donuts

Ingredients:

For the Donuts:

- 2 cups all-purpose flour
- 1/2 cup unsweetened cocoa powder
- 1 teaspoon baking powder
- 1/2 teaspoon baking soda
- 1/2 teaspoon salt
- 1 cup granulated sugar
- 2 large eggs
- 1 cup buttermilk
- 1/2 cup vegetable oil
- 1 teaspoon vanilla extract
- 2 tablespoons red food coloring

For the Cream Cheese Glaze:

- 4 ounces cream cheese, softened
- 1 cup powdered sugar
- 1 teaspoon vanilla extract
- 2-3 tablespoons milk

Instructions:

Preheat your oven to 350°F (175°C). Grease a donut pan.
In a medium bowl, whisk together the flour, cocoa powder, baking powder, baking soda, and salt.
In a large bowl, whisk together the sugar and eggs until well combined. Add the buttermilk, vegetable oil, vanilla extract, and red food coloring. Mix until smooth.
Gradually add the dry ingredients to the wet ingredients, mixing until just combined. Be careful not to overmix.
Spoon the batter into a piping bag or a zip-top bag with the corner snipped off. Pipe the batter into the prepared donut pan, filling each cavity about 2/3 full.

Bake for 12-15 minutes or until the donuts are firm and a toothpick inserted into the center comes out clean.

While the donuts are baking, prepare the cream cheese glaze. In a bowl, beat together the softened cream cheese, powdered sugar, vanilla extract, and enough milk to achieve a smooth glaze consistency.

Once the donuts are out of the oven and slightly cooled, dip each donut into the cream cheese glaze, ensuring they are well coated.

Place the glazed donuts on a wire rack to allow the glaze to set.

Enjoy your Red Velvet Donuts with a touch of cream cheese goodness!

These red velvet donuts are a delicious and visually stunning treat, perfect for special occasions or any time you crave the classic red velvet flavor.

Matcha Green Tea Donuts

Ingredients:

For the Donuts:

- 2 cups all-purpose flour
- 1/2 cup granulated sugar
- 2 teaspoons matcha green tea powder
- 1 1/2 teaspoons baking powder
- 1/2 teaspoon baking soda
- 1/2 teaspoon salt
- 2/3 cup buttermilk
- 2 large eggs
- 1/4 cup unsalted butter, melted
- 1 teaspoon vanilla extract

For the Matcha Glaze:

- 2 cups powdered sugar
- 2 tablespoons matcha green tea powder
- 3-4 tablespoons milk
- 1 teaspoon vanilla extract

Instructions:

Preheat your oven to 350°F (175°C). Grease a donut pan.
In a medium bowl, whisk together the flour, sugar, matcha powder, baking powder, baking soda, and salt.
In a separate bowl, whisk together the buttermilk, eggs, melted butter, and vanilla extract.
Add the wet ingredients to the dry ingredients and stir until just combined. Do not overmix.
Spoon the batter into a piping bag or a zip-top bag with the corner snipped off.
Pipe the batter into the prepared donut pan, filling each cavity about 2/3 full.
Bake for 12-15 minutes or until the donuts are firm and a toothpick inserted into the center comes out clean.

While the donuts are baking, prepare the matcha glaze. In a bowl, whisk together powdered sugar, matcha powder, milk, and vanilla extract until smooth.

Once the donuts are out of the oven and slightly cooled, dip each donut into the matcha glaze, ensuring they are well coated.

Place the glazed donuts on a wire rack to allow the glaze to set.

Enjoy your Matcha Green Tea Donuts with a cup of green tea for a delightful and unique treat!

These matcha donuts are a perfect choice for green tea enthusiasts and offer a delicious twist to the classic donut.

Strawberry Shortcake Donuts

Ingredients:

For the Donuts:

- 2 cups all-purpose flour
- 1/2 cup granulated sugar
- 1 1/2 teaspoons baking powder
- 1/2 teaspoon baking soda
- 1/2 teaspoon salt
- 1/2 cup buttermilk
- 2 large eggs
- 1/4 cup unsalted butter, melted
- 1 teaspoon vanilla extract
- 1 cup fresh strawberries, diced

For the Strawberry Glaze:

- 1 cup powdered sugar
- 1/2 cup fresh strawberries, pureed
- 1 teaspoon lemon juice

For the Whipped Cream Topping:

- 1 cup heavy cream
- 2 tablespoons powdered sugar
- 1 teaspoon vanilla extract

Instructions:

Preheat your oven to 350°F (175°C). Grease a donut pan.
In a medium bowl, whisk together the flour, sugar, baking powder, baking soda, and salt.
In a separate bowl, whisk together the buttermilk, eggs, melted butter, and vanilla extract.
Add the wet ingredients to the dry ingredients and stir until just combined. Gently fold in the diced strawberries.
Spoon the batter into a piping bag or a zip-top bag with the corner snipped off.
Pipe the batter into the prepared donut pan, filling each cavity about 2/3 full.

Bake for 12-15 minutes or until the donuts are firm and a toothpick inserted into the center comes out clean.

While the donuts are baking, prepare the strawberry glaze. In a bowl, whisk together powdered sugar, strawberry puree, and lemon juice until smooth.

Once the donuts are out of the oven and slightly cooled, dip each donut into the strawberry glaze, ensuring they are well coated.

For the whipped cream topping, whip the heavy cream, powdered sugar, and vanilla extract until stiff peaks form.

Just before serving, pipe or spoon a dollop of whipped cream onto each glazed donut.

Enjoy your Strawberry Shortcake Donuts with the perfect blend of strawberries, glaze, and whipped cream!

These Strawberry Shortcake Donuts are a delightful twist on the classic dessert, making them a perfect treat for brunch or any sweet occasion.

Cookies and Cream Donuts

Ingredients:

For the Donuts:

- 2 cups all-purpose flour
- 1/2 cup cocoa powder
- 1 1/2 teaspoons baking powder
- 1/2 teaspoon baking soda
- 1/2 teaspoon salt
- 1 cup granulated sugar
- 2 large eggs
- 1 cup buttermilk
- 1/4 cup vegetable oil
- 1 teaspoon vanilla extract
- 1 cup crushed chocolate sandwich cookies (like Oreo cookies)

For the Cookies and Cream Glaze:

- 1 1/2 cups powdered sugar
- 2 tablespoons milk
- 1/2 teaspoon vanilla extract
- 1/2 cup crushed chocolate sandwich cookies (for topping)

Instructions:

Preheat your oven to 350°F (175°C). Grease a donut pan.
In a medium bowl, whisk together the flour, cocoa powder, baking powder, baking soda, and salt.
In a separate bowl, whisk together the sugar, eggs, buttermilk, vegetable oil, and vanilla extract until well combined.
Add the wet ingredients to the dry ingredients and stir until just combined. Gently fold in the crushed chocolate sandwich cookies.
Spoon the batter into a piping bag or a zip-top bag with the corner snipped off.
Pipe the batter into the prepared donut pan, filling each cavity about 2/3 full.
Bake for 12-15 minutes or until the donuts are firm and a toothpick inserted into the center comes out clean.

While the donuts are baking, prepare the cookies and cream glaze. In a bowl, whisk together powdered sugar, milk, and vanilla extract until smooth.
Once the donuts are out of the oven and slightly cooled, dip each donut into the cookies and cream glaze, ensuring they are well coated.
Sprinkle the crushed chocolate sandwich cookies on top of the glazed donuts.
Place the glazed and topped donuts on a wire rack to allow the glaze to set.
Enjoy your Cookies and Cream Donuts with a perfect blend of chocolatey goodness and cookie crunch!

These donuts are a delightful indulgence for any cookies and cream lover. Perfect for breakfast, brunch, or a sweet treat at any time of the day.

Nutella-filled Donuts

Ingredients:

For the Donuts:

- 2 ¼ teaspoons (1 packet) active dry yeast
- 2 tablespoons warm water (about 110°F/43°C)
- 3/4 cup warm milk (about 110°F/43°C)
- 1/4 cup granulated sugar
- 1/4 cup unsalted butter, softened
- 1/2 teaspoon salt
- 1 large egg
- 3 cups all-purpose flour
- Vegetable oil (for frying)

For the Nutella Filling:

- 1/2 cup Nutella (or your favorite chocolate-hazelnut spread)

For the Coating:

- 1/2 cup powdered sugar

Instructions:

In a small bowl, combine the active dry yeast and warm water. Let it sit for 5 minutes until it becomes foamy.
In a large mixing bowl, combine the warm milk, sugar, softened butter, salt, and egg. Add the yeast mixture and mix well.
Gradually add the flour, one cup at a time, stirring until a soft dough forms.
Turn the dough onto a floured surface and knead for about 5 minutes until it becomes smooth and elastic.
Place the dough in a greased bowl, cover it with a clean cloth, and let it rise in a warm place for 1-1.5 hours or until doubled in size.
Roll out the dough on a floured surface to about 1/2-inch thickness. Cut out donut shapes using a donut cutter or two differently sized round cookie cutters.
Place a teaspoon-sized dollop of Nutella in the center of half of the dough circles.
Top each Nutella-filled circle with another dough circle, sealing the edges to create a filled donut.

Heat vegetable oil in a deep fryer or large, deep saucepan to 350°F (175°C).
Carefully place the filled donuts into the hot oil, frying each side until golden brown (about 1-2 minutes per side).
Remove the donuts with a slotted spoon and place them on a paper towel-lined plate to absorb excess oil.
Roll the warm Nutella-filled donuts in powdered sugar to coat them.
Allow the donuts to cool slightly before serving.
Enjoy your Nutella-filled Donuts with a gooey chocolate-hazelnut center!

These Nutella-filled donuts are a decadent and irresistible treat for all chocolate lovers. Enjoy them fresh and warm for the best experience!

Raspberry Jelly-filled Donuts

Ingredients:

For the Donuts:

- 2 ¼ teaspoons (1 packet) active dry yeast
- 2 tablespoons warm water (about 110°F/43°C)
- 3/4 cup warm milk (about 110°F/43°C)
- 1/4 cup granulated sugar
- 1/4 cup unsalted butter, softened
- 1/2 teaspoon salt
- 1 large egg
- 3 cups all-purpose flour
- Vegetable oil (for frying)

For the Raspberry Jelly Filling:

- 1/2 cup raspberry jam or jelly

For the Coating:

- 1/2 cup powdered sugar

Instructions:

In a small bowl, combine the active dry yeast and warm water. Let it sit for 5 minutes until it becomes foamy.
In a large mixing bowl, combine the warm milk, sugar, softened butter, salt, and egg. Add the yeast mixture and mix well.
Gradually add the flour, one cup at a time, stirring until a soft dough forms.
Turn the dough onto a floured surface and knead for about 5 minutes until it becomes smooth and elastic.
Place the dough in a greased bowl, cover it with a clean cloth, and let it rise in a warm place for 1-1.5 hours or until doubled in size.
Roll out the dough on a floured surface to about 1/2-inch thickness. Cut out donut shapes using a donut cutter or two differently sized round cookie cutters.

Heat vegetable oil in a deep fryer or large, deep saucepan to 350°F (175°C).
Carefully place the donuts into the hot oil, frying each side until golden brown (about 1-2 minutes per side).
Remove the donuts with a slotted spoon and place them on a paper towel-lined plate to absorb excess oil.
Once the donuts are cool enough to handle, fill a piping bag with a small tip with raspberry jam.
Insert the tip into the side of each donut and fill it with raspberry jam.
Roll the filled donuts in powdered sugar to coat them.
Allow the donuts to cool slightly before serving.
Enjoy your Raspberry Jelly-filled Donuts with a burst of sweet-tart raspberry goodness!

These jelly-filled donuts are a classic treat with a fruity twist. Perfect for breakfast, brunch, or anytime you want to indulge in a delightful and flavorful donut.

Coffee Glazed Donuts

Ingredients:

For the Donuts:

- 2 ¼ teaspoons (1 packet) active dry yeast
- 2 tablespoons warm water (about 110°F/43°C)
- 3/4 cup warm milk (about 110°F/43°C)
- 1/4 cup granulated sugar
- 1/4 cup unsalted butter, softened
- 1/2 teaspoon salt
- 1 large egg
- 3 cups all-purpose flour
- Vegetable oil (for frying)

For the Coffee Glaze:

- 1 1/2 cups powdered sugar
- 2 tablespoons brewed strong coffee, cooled
- 1/2 teaspoon vanilla extract

Instructions:

In a small bowl, combine the active dry yeast and warm water. Let it sit for 5 minutes until it becomes foamy.
In a large mixing bowl, combine the warm milk, sugar, softened butter, salt, and egg. Add the yeast mixture and mix well.
Gradually add the flour, one cup at a time, stirring until a soft dough forms.
Turn the dough onto a floured surface and knead for about 5 minutes until it becomes smooth and elastic.
Place the dough in a greased bowl, cover it with a clean cloth, and let it rise in a warm place for 1-1.5 hours or until doubled in size.
Roll out the dough on a floured surface to about 1/2-inch thickness. Cut out donut shapes using a donut cutter or two differently sized round cookie cutters.
Heat vegetable oil in a deep fryer or large, deep saucepan to 350°F (175°C).
Carefully place the donuts into the hot oil, frying each side until golden brown (about 1-2 minutes per side).

Remove the donuts with a slotted spoon and place them on a paper towel-lined plate to absorb excess oil.

In a bowl, whisk together powdered sugar, brewed coffee, and vanilla extract to make the coffee glaze.

Dip each donut into the coffee glaze, ensuring they are well coated, and place them on a wire rack to set.

Allow the glaze to set for about 15 minutes, and then your Coffee Glazed Donuts are ready to enjoy!

These coffee-glazed donuts are a perfect treat for coffee lovers, combining the bold flavors of coffee with the sweetness of the glaze. Enjoy with your favorite cup of coffee for an extra indulgent experience.

S'mores Donuts

Ingredients:

For the Donuts:

- 2 ¼ teaspoons (1 packet) active dry yeast
- 2 tablespoons warm water (about 110°F/43°C)
- 3/4 cup warm milk (about 110°F/43°C)
- 1/4 cup granulated sugar
- 1/4 cup unsalted butter, softened
- 1/2 teaspoon salt
- 1 large egg
- 3 cups all-purpose flour
- Vegetable oil (for frying)

For the Toppings:

- 1 cup chocolate chips or chunks
- 1 cup mini marshmallows
- 1 cup crushed graham crackers

Instructions:

In a small bowl, combine the active dry yeast and warm water. Let it sit for 5 minutes until it becomes foamy.

In a large mixing bowl, combine the warm milk, sugar, softened butter, salt, and egg. Add the yeast mixture and mix well.

Gradually add the flour, one cup at a time, stirring until a soft dough forms.

Turn the dough onto a floured surface and knead for about 5 minutes until it becomes smooth and elastic.

Place the dough in a greased bowl, cover it with a clean cloth, and let it rise in a warm place for 1-1.5 hours or until doubled in size.

Roll out the dough on a floured surface to about 1/2-inch thickness. Cut out donut shapes using a donut cutter or two differently sized round cookie cutters.

Heat vegetable oil in a deep fryer or large, deep saucepan to 350°F (175°C). Carefully place the donuts into the hot oil, frying each side until golden brown (about 1-2 minutes per side).

Remove the donuts with a slotted spoon and place them on a paper towel-lined plate to absorb excess oil.

While the donuts are still warm, sprinkle each with chocolate chips or chunks, mini marshmallows, and crushed graham crackers.

Optionally, you can use a kitchen torch to lightly toast the marshmallows for a true s'mores experience.

Allow the toppings to set for a few minutes, and then your S'mores Donuts are ready to be enjoyed!

These S'mores Donuts capture the essence of the beloved campfire treat in a delicious and portable form. Perfect for a sweet indulgence any time of the day!

Apple Cider Donuts

Ingredients:

For the Donuts:

- 2 cups apple cider
- 1/2 cup unsalted butter, softened
- 3/4 cup granulated sugar
- 2 large eggs
- 4 cups all-purpose flour
- 1 tablespoon baking powder
- 1/2 teaspoon baking soda
- 1/2 teaspoon salt
- 1 teaspoon ground cinnamon
- 1/2 teaspoon ground nutmeg
- 1/4 teaspoon ground cloves
- Vegetable oil (for frying)

For the Coating:

- 1 cup granulated sugar
- 1 tablespoon ground cinnamon

Instructions:

In a saucepan over medium heat, simmer the apple cider until it reduces to 1 cup. Allow it to cool.
In a large bowl, cream together the softened butter and sugar until light and fluffy. Add the eggs one at a time, beating well after each addition.
In a separate bowl, whisk together the reduced apple cider.
In another bowl, whisk together the flour, baking powder, baking soda, salt, cinnamon, nutmeg, and cloves.
Add the dry ingredients to the butter mixture alternately with the reduced apple cider, beginning and ending with the dry ingredients. Mix until just combined.
Cover the bowl with plastic wrap and refrigerate the dough for at least 1 hour or overnight.
On a floured surface, roll out the chilled dough to a 1/2-inch thickness.
Heat vegetable oil in a deep fryer or large, deep saucepan to 375°F (190°C).

Cut out donut shapes using a donut cutter or two differently sized round cookie cutters.

Carefully place the donuts into the hot oil, frying each side until golden brown (about 1-2 minutes per side). Fry in batches to avoid overcrowding.

Remove the donuts with a slotted spoon and place them on a paper towel-lined plate to absorb excess oil.

In a bowl, mix together granulated sugar and ground cinnamon for the coating.

While the donuts are still warm, roll them in the cinnamon-sugar mixture to coat them.

Allow the donuts to cool slightly before serving.

Enjoy your Apple Cider Donuts with the warm, comforting flavors of fall!

These Apple Cider Donuts are a delicious autumn treat, perfect for enjoying with a cup of hot apple cider or your favorite fall beverage.

Coconut Lime Donuts

Ingredients:

For the Donuts:

- 2 cups all-purpose flour
- 1 cup granulated sugar
- 1 1/2 teaspoons baking powder
- 1/2 teaspoon baking soda
- 1/2 teaspoon salt
- 1 cup coconut milk
- 1/4 cup vegetable oil
- 2 large eggs
- Zest of 2 limes
- 2 tablespoons fresh lime juice
- 1 teaspoon vanilla extract

For the Coconut Lime Glaze:

- 1 1/2 cups powdered sugar
- 3 tablespoons coconut milk
- 2 tablespoons fresh lime juice
- Shredded coconut, for topping (optional)

Instructions:

Preheat your oven to 350°F (175°C). Grease a donut pan.
In a large bowl, whisk together the flour, sugar, baking powder, baking soda, and salt.
In a separate bowl, whisk together the coconut milk, vegetable oil, eggs, lime zest, lime juice, and vanilla extract.
Add the wet ingredients to the dry ingredients and stir until just combined. Do not overmix.
Spoon the batter into a piping bag or a zip-top bag with the corner snipped off.
Pipe the batter into the prepared donut pan, filling each cavity about 2/3 full.
Bake for 12-15 minutes or until the donuts are golden brown and a toothpick inserted into the center comes out clean.

While the donuts are baking, prepare the coconut lime glaze. In a bowl, whisk together powdered sugar, coconut milk, and lime juice until smooth.
Once the donuts are out of the oven and slightly cooled, dip each donut into the coconut lime glaze, ensuring they are well coated.
If desired, sprinkle shredded coconut on top of the glazed donuts for added texture.
Place the glazed and topped donuts on a wire rack to allow the glaze to set.
Enjoy your Coconut Lime Donuts with a burst of tropical and citrus flavors!

These donuts are a perfect choice for those who love the combination of coconut and lime. They're a delightful treat for breakfast or a sweet snack with a cup of tea or coffee.

Pistachio Glazed Donuts

Ingredients:

For the Donuts:

- 2 cups all-purpose flour
- 1 cup granulated sugar
- 1 1/2 teaspoons baking powder
- 1/2 teaspoon baking soda
- 1/2 teaspoon salt
- 1 cup buttermilk
- 2 large eggs
- 1/4 cup unsalted butter, melted
- 1/2 cup shelled pistachios, finely ground

For the Pistachio Glaze:

- 1 cup powdered sugar
- 2 tablespoons pistachio paste or finely ground pistachios
- 2-3 tablespoons milk
- Chopped pistachios for topping (optional)

Instructions:

Preheat your oven to 350°F (175°C). Grease a donut pan.
In a large bowl, whisk together the flour, sugar, baking powder, baking soda, and salt.
In a separate bowl, whisk together the buttermilk, eggs, melted butter, and finely ground pistachios.
Add the wet ingredients to the dry ingredients and stir until just combined. Do not overmix.
Spoon the batter into a piping bag or a zip-top bag with the corner snipped off.
Pipe the batter into the prepared donut pan, filling each cavity about 2/3 full.
Bake for 12-15 minutes or until the donuts are golden brown and a toothpick inserted into the center comes out clean.

While the donuts are baking, prepare the pistachio glaze. In a bowl, whisk together powdered sugar, pistachio paste or ground pistachios, and enough milk to achieve a smooth glaze consistency.

Once the donuts are out of the oven and slightly cooled, dip each donut into the pistachio glaze, ensuring they are well coated.

If desired, sprinkle chopped pistachios on top of the glazed donuts for added texture.

Place the glazed and topped donuts on a wire rack to allow the glaze to set.

Enjoy your Pistachio Glazed Donuts with a delightful nutty flavor!

These donuts offer a unique twist with the rich and distinctive taste of pistachios. They make for a delightful treat for breakfast or dessert, especially for pistachio lovers!

Mocha Almond Fudge Donuts

Ingredients:

For the Donuts:

- 2 cups all-purpose flour
- 1 cup granulated sugar
- 1/2 cup unsweetened cocoa powder
- 1 1/2 teaspoons baking powder
- 1/2 teaspoon baking soda
- 1/2 teaspoon salt
- 1 cup strong brewed coffee, cooled
- 1/2 cup vegetable oil
- 2 large eggs
- 1 teaspoon vanilla extract
- 1/2 cup chopped almonds (optional)

For the Mocha Almond Fudge Glaze:

- 1 cup powdered sugar
- 2 tablespoons unsweetened cocoa powder
- 2 tablespoons strong brewed coffee, cooled
- 1/2 teaspoon almond extract
- 1/4 cup chopped almonds for topping (optional)

Instructions:

Preheat your oven to 350°F (175°C). Grease a donut pan.
In a large bowl, whisk together the flour, sugar, cocoa powder, baking powder, baking soda, and salt.
In another bowl, whisk together the cooled brewed coffee, vegetable oil, eggs, and vanilla extract.
Add the wet ingredients to the dry ingredients and stir until just combined. Do not overmix.
If desired, fold in the chopped almonds into the batter.
Spoon the batter into a piping bag or a zip-top bag with the corner snipped off.
Pipe the batter into the prepared donut pan, filling each cavity about 2/3 full.

Bake for 12-15 minutes or until the donuts are firm and a toothpick inserted into the center comes out clean.

While the donuts are baking, prepare the mocha almond fudge glaze. In a bowl, whisk together powdered sugar, cocoa powder, brewed coffee, and almond extract until smooth.

Once the donuts are out of the oven and slightly cooled, dip each donut into the mocha almond fudge glaze, ensuring they are well coated.

If desired, sprinkle chopped almonds on top of the glazed donuts for added texture.

Place the glazed and topped donuts on a wire rack to allow the glaze to set.

Enjoy your Mocha Almond Fudge Donuts with a delicious combination of mocha, chocolate, and almonds!

These donuts are perfect for those who love the classic pairing of coffee and chocolate with an added crunch of almonds. They make for a delightful dessert or a special treat for breakfast.

Churro Donuts

Ingredients:

For the Donuts:

- 2 cups all-purpose flour
- 1 1/2 teaspoons baking powder
- 1/2 teaspoon baking soda
- 1/2 teaspoon salt
- 1 teaspoon ground cinnamon
- 2/3 cup granulated sugar
- 2 large eggs
- 1 cup buttermilk
- 1/4 cup unsalted butter, melted
- 1 teaspoon vanilla extract

For the Cinnamon Sugar Coating:

- 1/2 cup unsalted butter, melted
- 1 cup granulated sugar
- 2 teaspoons ground cinnamon

Instructions:

Preheat your oven to 350°F (175°C). Grease a donut pan.
In a large bowl, whisk together the flour, baking powder, baking soda, salt, and ground cinnamon.
In another bowl, whisk together the sugar, eggs, buttermilk, melted butter, and vanilla extract.
Add the wet ingredients to the dry ingredients and stir until just combined. Do not overmix.
Spoon the batter into a piping bag or a zip-top bag with the corner snipped off.
Pipe the batter into the prepared donut pan, filling each cavity about 2/3 full.
Bake for 12-15 minutes or until the donuts are firm and a toothpick inserted into the center comes out clean.
While the donuts are baking, prepare the cinnamon sugar coating. In a bowl, combine granulated sugar and ground cinnamon.

Once the donuts are out of the oven and slightly cooled, dip each donut into the melted butter and then roll them in the cinnamon sugar mixture, ensuring they are well coated.

Place the coated donuts on a wire rack to allow excess coating to drip off and let them cool completely.

Enjoy your Churro Donuts with a perfect blend of cinnamon and sugar goodness!

These Churro Donuts bring the beloved flavors of churros into a delightful donut form. They are perfect for breakfast, brunch, or any time you crave a sweet and crunchy treat.

Chocolate Mint Donuts

Ingredients:

For the Donuts:

- 1 cup all-purpose flour
- 1/4 cup unsweetened cocoa powder
- 1/2 teaspoon baking powder
- 1/4 teaspoon baking soda
- 1/4 teaspoon salt
- 1/2 cup granulated sugar
- 1/4 cup vegetable oil
- 1/2 cup buttermilk
- 1 large egg
- 1 teaspoon peppermint extract
- 1/2 teaspoon vanilla extract

For the Mint Chocolate Glaze:

- 1 cup powdered sugar
- 2 tablespoons unsweetened cocoa powder
- 2-3 tablespoons milk
- 1/4 teaspoon peppermint extract
- Green food coloring (optional)
- Crushed candy canes or mint candies for topping (optional)

Instructions:

Preheat your oven to 350°F (175°C). Grease a donut pan.
In a large bowl, whisk together the flour, cocoa powder, baking powder, baking soda, and salt.
In a separate bowl, whisk together the sugar, vegetable oil, buttermilk, egg, peppermint extract, and vanilla extract until well combined.
Add the wet ingredients to the dry ingredients and stir until just combined. Do not overmix.
Spoon the batter into a piping bag or a zip-top bag with the corner snipped off.
Pipe the batter into the prepared donut pan, filling each cavity about 2/3 full.

Bake for 10-12 minutes or until a toothpick inserted into the center comes out clean.

While the donuts are baking, prepare the mint chocolate glaze. In a bowl, whisk together powdered sugar, cocoa powder, milk, peppermint extract, and green food coloring (if using) until smooth.

Once the donuts are out of the oven and slightly cooled, dip each donut into the mint chocolate glaze, ensuring they are well coated.

Place the glazed donuts on a wire rack to allow excess glaze to drip off.

Optionally, sprinkle crushed candy canes or mint candies on top of the glazed donuts for a festive touch.

Allow the glaze to set for about 15 minutes before serving.

Enjoy your homemade Chocolate Mint Donuts with a delightful blend of rich chocolate and refreshing mint flavor!

These donuts are a perfect treat for any occasion, especially during the holiday season. Enjoy!

Pina Colada Donuts

Ingredients:

For the Donuts:

- 1 1/2 cups all-purpose flour
- 1/2 cup granulated sugar
- 1 1/2 teaspoons baking powder
- 1/4 teaspoon baking soda
- 1/4 teaspoon salt
- 1/2 cup crushed pineapple, drained
- 1/2 cup coconut milk
- 1/4 cup unsalted butter, melted
- 1 large egg
- 1 teaspoon vanilla extract
- Zest of 1 lime (optional)

For the Coconut Glaze:

- 1 cup powdered sugar
- 2-3 tablespoons coconut milk
- 1/2 cup shredded coconut, toasted (for topping)

Instructions:

Preheat your oven to 350°F (175°C). Grease a donut pan.
In a large bowl, whisk together the flour, sugar, baking powder, baking soda, and salt.
In another bowl, mix together the crushed pineapple, coconut milk, melted butter, egg, vanilla extract, and lime zest (if using).
Add the wet ingredients to the dry ingredients and stir until just combined. Do not overmix.
Spoon the batter into a piping bag or a zip-top bag with the corner snipped off.
Pipe the batter into the prepared donut pan, filling each cavity about 2/3 full.
Bake for 12-15 minutes or until the donuts are firm and a toothpick inserted into the center comes out clean.

While the donuts are baking, prepare the coconut glaze. In a bowl, whisk together powdered sugar and coconut milk until smooth.

Once the donuts are out of the oven and slightly cooled, dip each donut into the coconut glaze, ensuring they are well coated.

Sprinkle toasted shredded coconut on top of the glazed donuts for added flavor and texture.

Place the glazed and topped donuts on a wire rack to allow the glaze to set.

Enjoy your Pina Colada Donuts with the tropical goodness of pineapple and coconut!

These donuts are a perfect treat for a tropical escape. The combination of pineapple, coconut, and a hint of lime makes them a delightful choice for breakfast or dessert.

Brown Butter Bourbon Donuts

Ingredients:

For the Donuts:

- 2 cups all-purpose flour
- 1 1/2 teaspoons baking powder
- 1/2 teaspoon baking soda
- 1/2 teaspoon salt
- 1/2 cup unsalted butter
- 1 cup granulated sugar
- 2 large eggs
- 1 teaspoon vanilla extract
- 1/2 cup buttermilk
- 2 tablespoons bourbon

For the Glaze:

- 1/4 cup unsalted butter
- 2 cups powdered sugar
- 3 tablespoons bourbon
- 1 teaspoon vanilla extract
- Pinch of salt
- Chopped pecans or walnuts for garnish (optional)

Instructions:

For the Donuts:

Preheat your oven to 350°F (175°C). Grease a donut pan.
In a medium saucepan over medium heat, melt the butter. Once melted, continue cooking, stirring frequently until the butter turns brown and gives off a nutty aroma. Be careful not to burn it. Remove from heat and let it cool.
In a large mixing bowl, whisk together the flour, baking powder, baking soda, and salt.
In another bowl, combine the cooled brown butter and sugar. Mix until well combined.
Add the eggs one at a time, beating well after each addition. Stir in the vanilla extract.

Alternately add the flour mixture and buttermilk to the wet ingredients, beginning and ending with the flour mixture. Mix until just combined.

Add the bourbon and mix until smooth.

Spoon the batter into a piping bag or a zip-top bag with the corner snipped off. Pipe the batter into the prepared donut pan, filling each cavity about 2/3 full.

Bake for 12-15 minutes or until a toothpick inserted into the center comes out clean.

Allow the donuts to cool in the pan for a few minutes before transferring them to a wire rack to cool completely.

For the Glaze:

In a small saucepan, melt the butter over medium heat. Continue cooking until the butter turns brown and gives off a nutty aroma.

In a mixing bowl, combine the powdered sugar, browned butter, bourbon, vanilla extract, and a pinch of salt. Whisk until smooth.

Dip each cooled donut into the glaze, ensuring they are well coated.

Optionally, sprinkle chopped pecans or walnuts on top of the glazed donuts.

Allow the glaze to set for a few minutes before serving.

Enjoy your Brown Butter Bourbon Donuts with the rich and warm flavors of browned butter and bourbon!

These donuts are perfect for a special occasion or a delightful treat for those who appreciate the combination of brown butter and bourbon.

Almond Joy Donuts

Ingredients:

For the Donuts:

- 1 cup all-purpose flour
- 1/3 cup unsweetened cocoa powder
- 1/2 teaspoon baking powder
- 1/4 teaspoon baking soda
- 1/4 teaspoon salt
- 1/2 cup granulated sugar
- 1/4 cup vegetable oil
- 1/2 cup buttermilk
- 1 large egg
- 1 teaspoon vanilla extract
- 1/4 cup shredded coconut (sweetened or unsweetened)

For the Toppings:

- 1/2 cup shredded coconut, toasted
- 1/2 cup sliced almonds, toasted
- 1/2 cup chocolate chips, melted

Instructions:

Preheat your oven to 350°F (175°C). Grease a donut pan.
In a large bowl, whisk together the flour, cocoa powder, baking powder, baking soda, and salt.
In another bowl, whisk together the sugar, vegetable oil, buttermilk, egg, and vanilla extract until well combined.
Add the wet ingredients to the dry ingredients and stir until just combined. Do not overmix.
Fold in the shredded coconut.
Spoon the batter into a piping bag or a zip-top bag with the corner snipped off.
Pipe the batter into the prepared donut pan, filling each cavity about 2/3 full.
Bake for 10-12 minutes or until the donuts are firm and a toothpick inserted into the center comes out clean.

Allow the donuts to cool in the pan for a few minutes before transferring them to a wire rack to cool completely.

While the donuts are cooling, toast the shredded coconut and sliced almonds in a dry skillet over medium heat until lightly browned.

Once the donuts are cooled, dip the tops into the melted chocolate, allowing any excess to drip off.

Immediately sprinkle the toasted coconut and sliced almonds on top of the chocolate-dipped donuts.

Allow the chocolate to set before serving.

Enjoy your Almond Joy Donuts with the perfect combination of coconut, almonds, and chocolate!

These donuts capture the delicious flavors of the classic Almond Joy candy bar in a delightful baked treat. Perfect for satisfying your sweet tooth!

Funfetti Donuts

Ingredients:

For the Donuts:

- 2 cups all-purpose flour
- 1 cup granulated sugar
- 1 1/2 teaspoons baking powder
- 1/2 teaspoon baking soda
- 1/2 teaspoon salt
- 1 cup buttermilk
- 2 large eggs
- 1/4 cup unsalted butter, melted
- 2 teaspoons vanilla extract
- 1/2 cup rainbow sprinkles

For the Glaze:

- 2 cups powdered sugar
- 1/4 cup milk
- 1 teaspoon vanilla extract
- Additional rainbow sprinkles for topping

Instructions:

Preheat your oven to 350°F (175°C). Grease a donut pan.
In a large bowl, whisk together the flour, sugar, baking powder, baking soda, and salt.
In another bowl, whisk together the buttermilk, eggs, melted butter, and vanilla extract until well combined.
Add the wet ingredients to the dry ingredients and stir until just combined. Do not overmix.
Fold in the rainbow sprinkles until evenly distributed throughout the batter.
Spoon the batter into a piping bag or a zip-top bag with the corner snipped off.
Pipe the batter into the prepared donut pan, filling each cavity about 2/3 full.
Bake for 10-12 minutes or until the donuts are firm and a toothpick inserted into the center comes out clean.

Allow the donuts to cool in the pan for a few minutes before transferring them to a wire rack to cool completely.

In a bowl, whisk together the powdered sugar, milk, and vanilla extract to create the glaze.

Once the donuts are completely cooled, dip each donut into the glaze, ensuring they are well coated.

Immediately sprinkle additional rainbow sprinkles on top of the glazed donuts.

Allow the glaze to set for a few minutes before serving.

Enjoy your Funfetti Donuts with the burst of color and sweetness from the sprinkles!

These Funfetti Donuts are a cheerful and delicious way to start your day or add a festive touch to any occasion. They're sure to bring a smile to both kids and adults alike!

Cherry Cheesecake Donuts

Ingredients:

For the Donuts:

- 1 1/2 cups all-purpose flour
- 1/2 cup granulated sugar
- 1 1/2 teaspoons baking powder
- 1/4 teaspoon baking soda
- 1/4 teaspoon salt
- 1/2 cup buttermilk
- 1/4 cup unsalted butter, melted
- 1 large egg
- 1 teaspoon vanilla extract

For the Cheesecake Filling:

- 8 oz cream cheese, softened
- 1/4 cup granulated sugar
- 1 large egg yolk
- 1/2 teaspoon vanilla extract

For the Cherry Topping:

- 1 cup cherry pie filling

Instructions:

For the Donuts:

> Preheat your oven to 350°F (175°C). Grease a donut pan.
> In a large bowl, whisk together the flour, sugar, baking powder, baking soda, and salt.
> In another bowl, whisk together the buttermilk, melted butter, egg, and vanilla extract.
> Add the wet ingredients to the dry ingredients and stir until just combined. Do not overmix.
> Spoon the batter into a piping bag or a zip-top bag with the corner snipped off.
> Pipe the batter into the prepared donut pan, filling each cavity about 2/3 full.

In a separate bowl, prepare the cheesecake filling by mixing the softened cream cheese, sugar, egg yolk, and vanilla extract until smooth.

Spoon a small amount of cheesecake filling onto the center of each donut batter in the pan.

Bake for 12-15 minutes or until the donuts are firm and a toothpick inserted into the donut (not the filling) comes out clean.

Allow the donuts to cool in the pan for a few minutes before transferring them to a wire rack to cool completely.

For the Cherry Topping:

Once the donuts are cooled, spoon a dollop of cherry pie filling onto the top of each donut.

Gently spread the cherry pie filling to cover the surface of the donuts.

Allow the cherry topping to set for a few minutes before serving.

Enjoy your Cherry Cheesecake Donuts with the perfect combination of creamy cheesecake, sweet cherries, and soft donut goodness!

These donuts offer a delightful twist on classic cheesecake by incorporating the flavors of cherry pie filling. They're a wonderful treat for dessert or a special brunch.

Salted Caramel Pretzel Donuts

Ingredients:

For the Donuts:

- 1 1/2 cups all-purpose flour
- 1/2 cup granulated sugar
- 1 1/2 teaspoons baking powder
- 1/4 teaspoon baking soda
- 1/4 teaspoon salt
- 1/2 cup buttermilk
- 1/4 cup unsalted butter, melted
- 1 large egg
- 1 teaspoon vanilla extract

For the Salted Caramel Glaze:

- 1/2 cup unsalted butter
- 1 cup packed brown sugar
- 1/2 cup heavy cream
- 1/2 teaspoon sea salt (adjust to taste)

For the Pretzel Topping:

- Pretzel twists or sticks, crushed

Instructions:

For the Donuts:

Preheat your oven to 350°F (175°C). Grease a donut pan.
In a large bowl, whisk together the flour, sugar, baking powder, baking soda, and salt.
In another bowl, whisk together the buttermilk, melted butter, egg, and vanilla extract.
Add the wet ingredients to the dry ingredients and stir until just combined. Do not overmix.
Spoon the batter into a piping bag or a zip-top bag with the corner snipped off.
Pipe the batter into the prepared donut pan, filling each cavity about 2/3 full.

Bake for 10-12 minutes or until the donuts are firm and a toothpick inserted into the center comes out clean.

Allow the donuts to cool in the pan for a few minutes before transferring them to a wire rack to cool completely.

For the Salted Caramel Glaze:

In a saucepan over medium heat, melt the butter.

Stir in the brown sugar and heavy cream. Bring the mixture to a gentle boil, stirring continuously.

Let it simmer for 2-3 minutes until the sauce thickens.

Remove the pan from heat and stir in the sea salt. Allow the caramel to cool slightly.

Assembly:

Dip the tops of each cooled donut into the salted caramel glaze, ensuring they are well coated.

Immediately sprinkle the crushed pretzels on top of the glazed donuts.

Allow the glaze to set for a few minutes before serving.

Enjoy your Salted Caramel Pretzel Donuts with the perfect combination of sweet, salty, and crunchy goodness!

These donuts are a delightful treat for those who enjoy the irresistible combination of salted caramel and pretzels. Perfect for dessert or a special brunch!

Double Chocolate Chunk Donuts

Ingredients:

For the Donuts:

- 1 cup all-purpose flour
- 1/4 cup unsweetened cocoa powder
- 1/2 teaspoon baking powder
- 1/4 teaspoon baking soda
- 1/4 teaspoon salt
- 1/2 cup granulated sugar
- 1/4 cup unsalted butter, melted
- 1/2 cup buttermilk
- 1 large egg
- 1 teaspoon vanilla extract
- 1/2 cup chocolate chunks or chocolate chips

For the Chocolate Glaze:

- 1/2 cup chocolate chips
- 2 tablespoons unsalted butter
- 2 tablespoons corn syrup or honey
- 1/2 teaspoon vanilla extract

Instructions:

For the Donuts:

Preheat your oven to 350°F (175°C). Grease a donut pan.
In a large bowl, whisk together the flour, cocoa powder, baking powder, baking soda, and salt.
In another bowl, mix together the granulated sugar, melted butter, buttermilk, egg, and vanilla extract.
Add the wet ingredients to the dry ingredients and stir until just combined. Do not overmix.
Fold in the chocolate chunks or chocolate chips.
Spoon the batter into a piping bag or a zip-top bag with the corner snipped off.
Pipe the batter into the prepared donut pan, filling each cavity about 2/3 full.

Bake for 10-12 minutes or until the donuts are firm and a toothpick inserted into the center comes out clean.
Allow the donuts to cool in the pan for a few minutes before transferring them to a wire rack to cool completely.

For the Chocolate Glaze:

In a small saucepan over low heat, melt the chocolate chips, butter, and corn syrup or honey, stirring until smooth.
Remove the pan from heat and stir in the vanilla extract.

Assembly:

Dip the tops of each cooled donut into the chocolate glaze, ensuring they are well coated.
Place the glazed donuts on a wire rack to allow excess glaze to drip off.
Allow the glaze to set for a few minutes before serving.
Enjoy your Double Chocolate Chunk Donuts with the perfect combination of rich, chocolaty flavor and melty chocolate chunks!

These donuts are a chocolate lover's dream, with double the chocolate goodness from the donut batter and the luscious chocolate glaze. Perfect for satisfying your sweet tooth!

Raspberry White Chocolate Donuts

Ingredients:

For the Donuts:

- 1 1/2 cups all-purpose flour
- 1/2 cup granulated sugar
- 1 1/2 teaspoons baking powder
- 1/4 teaspoon baking soda
- 1/4 teaspoon salt
- 1/2 cup buttermilk
- 1/4 cup unsalted butter, melted
- 1/2 cup raspberry puree (fresh or frozen raspberries blended until smooth)
- 1 large egg
- 1 teaspoon vanilla extract
- 1/2 cup white chocolate chips

For the White Chocolate Glaze:

- 1/2 cup white chocolate chips
- 2 tablespoons heavy cream
- 1/2 teaspoon vanilla extract

Fresh raspberries for topping (optional)

Instructions:

For the Donuts:

Preheat your oven to 350°F (175°C). Grease a donut pan.
In a large bowl, whisk together the flour, sugar, baking powder, baking soda, and salt.
In another bowl, mix together the buttermilk, melted butter, raspberry puree, egg, and vanilla extract.

Add the wet ingredients to the dry ingredients and stir until just combined. Do not overmix.

Fold in the white chocolate chips.

Spoon the batter into a piping bag or a zip-top bag with the corner snipped off.

Pipe the batter into the prepared donut pan, filling each cavity about 2/3 full.

Bake for 10-12 minutes or until the donuts are firm and a toothpick inserted into the center comes out clean.

Allow the donuts to cool in the pan for a few minutes before transferring them to a wire rack to cool completely.

For the White Chocolate Glaze:

In a heatproof bowl, melt the white chocolate chips and heavy cream together, either in a microwave or using a double boiler, stirring until smooth.

Stir in the vanilla extract.

Assembly:

Dip the tops of each cooled donut into the white chocolate glaze, ensuring they are well coated.

Place the glazed donuts on a wire rack to allow excess glaze to drip off.

Optionally, top each glazed donut with fresh raspberries for added freshness and flavor.

Allow the glaze to set for a few minutes before serving.

Enjoy your Raspberry White Chocolate Donuts with the delightful combination of tart raspberries and sweet white chocolate!

These donuts are a perfect balance of fruity and sweet, making them a delicious treat for breakfast or dessert.

Orange Creamsicle Donuts

Ingredients:

For the Donuts:

- 1 1/2 cups all-purpose flour
- 1/2 cup granulated sugar
- 1 1/2 teaspoons baking powder
- 1/4 teaspoon baking soda
- 1/4 teaspoon salt
- 1/2 cup buttermilk
- 1/4 cup unsalted butter, melted
- 1/4 cup freshly squeezed orange juice
- Zest of 1 orange
- 1 large egg
- 1 teaspoon vanilla extract

For the Vanilla Glaze:

- 1 cup powdered sugar
- 2 tablespoons milk
- 1/2 teaspoon vanilla extract

Additional orange zest for topping (optional)

Instructions:

For the Donuts:

> Preheat your oven to 350°F (175°C). Grease a donut pan.
> In a large bowl, whisk together the flour, sugar, baking powder, baking soda, and salt.
> In another bowl, mix together the buttermilk, melted butter, orange juice, orange zest, egg, and vanilla extract.
> Add the wet ingredients to the dry ingredients and stir until just combined. Do not overmix.
> Spoon the batter into a piping bag or a zip-top bag with the corner snipped off.
> Pipe the batter into the prepared donut pan, filling each cavity about 2/3 full.

Bake for 10-12 minutes or until the donuts are firm and a toothpick inserted into the center comes out clean.

Allow the donuts to cool in the pan for a few minutes before transferring them to a wire rack to cool completely.

For the Vanilla Glaze:

In a bowl, whisk together the powdered sugar, milk, and vanilla extract until smooth.

Assembly:

Dip the tops of each cooled donut into the vanilla glaze, ensuring they are well coated.

Optionally, sprinkle additional orange zest on top of the glazed donuts for extra citrusy flavor.

Allow the glaze to set for a few minutes before serving.

Enjoy your Orange Creamsicle Donuts with the perfect blend of orange citrus and creamy vanilla!

These donuts capture the refreshing and nostalgic flavor of orange creamsicles, making them a delightful choice for breakfast or a sweet treat.

Peanut Butter Cup Donuts

Ingredients:

For the Donuts:

- 1 cup all-purpose flour
- 1/4 cup cocoa powder
- 1/2 teaspoon baking powder
- 1/4 teaspoon baking soda
- 1/4 teaspoon salt
- 1/2 cup granulated sugar
- 1/4 cup creamy peanut butter
- 1/4 cup unsalted butter, melted
- 1/2 cup buttermilk
- 1 large egg
- 1 teaspoon vanilla extract
- 1/2 cup chopped peanut butter cups

For the Chocolate Glaze:

- 1/2 cup chocolate chips
- 2 tablespoons unsalted butter
- 2 tablespoons corn syrup or honey
- Chopped peanuts for topping (optional)

Instructions:

For the Donuts:

Preheat your oven to 350°F (175°C). Grease a donut pan.
In a large bowl, whisk together the flour, cocoa powder, baking powder, baking soda, and salt.
In another bowl, mix together the granulated sugar, peanut butter, melted butter, buttermilk, egg, and vanilla extract.
Add the wet ingredients to the dry ingredients and stir until just combined. Do not overmix.
Fold in the chopped peanut butter cups.
Spoon the batter into a piping bag or a zip-top bag with the corner snipped off.
Pipe the batter into the prepared donut pan, filling each cavity about 2/3 full.

Bake for 10-12 minutes or until the donuts are firm and a toothpick inserted into the center comes out clean.

Allow the donuts to cool in the pan for a few minutes before transferring them to a wire rack to cool completely.

For the Chocolate Glaze:

In a heatproof bowl, melt the chocolate chips, butter, and corn syrup or honey, stirring until smooth.

Assembly:

Dip the tops of each cooled donut into the chocolate glaze, ensuring they are well coated.

Optionally, sprinkle chopped peanuts on top of the glazed donuts for added crunch.

Allow the glaze to set for a few minutes before serving.

Enjoy your Peanut Butter Cup Donuts with the perfect combination of peanut butter and chocolate!

These donuts are a delightful treat for peanut butter and chocolate lovers, combining the classic flavors of peanut butter cups in a baked donut form. Perfect for indulging your sweet cravings!

Blackberry Lavender Donuts

Ingredients:

For the Donuts:

- 1 1/2 cups all-purpose flour
- 1/2 cup granulated sugar
- 1 1/2 teaspoons baking powder
- 1/4 teaspoon baking soda
- 1/4 teaspoon salt
- 1/2 cup buttermilk
- 1/4 cup unsalted butter, melted
- 1/2 cup blackberry puree (fresh or frozen blackberries blended until smooth)
- 1 large egg
- 1 teaspoon vanilla extract
- 1 teaspoon dried culinary lavender, finely chopped

For the Blackberry Glaze:

- 1 cup powdered sugar
- 2 tablespoons blackberry puree
- 1/2 teaspoon dried culinary lavender, finely chopped

Instructions:

For the Donuts:

Preheat your oven to 350°F (175°C). Grease a donut pan.
In a large bowl, whisk together the flour, sugar, baking powder, baking soda, and salt.
In another bowl, mix together the buttermilk, melted butter, blackberry puree, egg, vanilla extract, and chopped lavender.
Add the wet ingredients to the dry ingredients and stir until just combined. Do not overmix.
Spoon the batter into a piping bag or a zip-top bag with the corner snipped off.
Pipe the batter into the prepared donut pan, filling each cavity about 2/3 full.

Bake for 10-12 minutes or until the donuts are firm and a toothpick inserted into the center comes out clean.

Allow the donuts to cool in the pan for a few minutes before transferring them to a wire rack to cool completely.

For the Blackberry Glaze:

In a bowl, whisk together the powdered sugar, blackberry puree, and chopped lavender until smooth.

Assembly:

Dip the tops of each cooled donut into the blackberry glaze, ensuring they are well coated.

Place the glazed donuts on a wire rack to allow excess glaze to drip off.

Allow the glaze to set for a few minutes before serving.

Enjoy your Blackberry Lavender Donuts with the delightful combination of fruity blackberries and aromatic lavender!

These donuts offer a unique and elegant flavor profile, making them a perfect choice for a special breakfast or dessert. The blackberry and lavender combination creates a beautifully fragrant and tasty treat.

Blueberry Lemon Glazed Donuts

Ingredients:

For the Donuts:

- 1 1/2 cups all-purpose flour
- 1/2 cup granulated sugar
- 1 1/2 teaspoons baking powder
- 1/4 teaspoon baking soda
- 1/4 teaspoon salt
- 1/2 cup buttermilk
- 1/4 cup unsalted butter, melted
- Zest of 1 lemon
- 1/2 cup blueberries (fresh or frozen)

For the Lemon Glaze:

- 1 cup powdered sugar
- 2 tablespoons fresh lemon juice
- Zest of 1 lemon

Instructions:

For the Donuts:

Preheat your oven to 350°F (175°C). Grease a donut pan.
In a large bowl, whisk together the flour, sugar, baking powder, baking soda, and salt.
In another bowl, mix together the buttermilk, melted butter, and lemon zest.
Add the wet ingredients to the dry ingredients and stir until just combined. Do not overmix.
Gently fold in the blueberries.
Spoon the batter into a piping bag or a zip-top bag with the corner snipped off.
Pipe the batter into the prepared donut pan, filling each cavity about 2/3 full.
Bake for 10-12 minutes or until the donuts are firm and a toothpick inserted into the center comes out clean.

Allow the donuts to cool in the pan for a few minutes before transferring them to a wire rack to cool completely.

For the Lemon Glaze:

In a bowl, whisk together the powdered sugar, fresh lemon juice, and lemon zest until smooth.

Assembly:

Dip the tops of each cooled donut into the lemon glaze, ensuring they are well coated.
Place the glazed donuts on a wire rack to allow excess glaze to drip off.
Allow the glaze to set for a few minutes before serving.
Enjoy your Blueberry Lemon Glazed Donuts with the perfect combination of sweet blueberries and zesty lemon!

These donuts offer a burst of fruity freshness, making them a delightful choice for breakfast or a summery treat. The blueberry and lemon pairing creates a harmonious blend of flavors.

Carrot Cake Donuts

Ingredients:

For the Donuts:

- 1 cup all-purpose flour
- 1/2 cup granulated sugar
- 1/2 teaspoon baking powder
- 1/4 teaspoon baking soda
- 1/4 teaspoon salt
- 1/2 teaspoon ground cinnamon
- 1/4 teaspoon ground nutmeg
- 1/4 cup vegetable oil
- 1 large egg
- 1/2 cup finely grated carrot
- 1/4 cup crushed pineapple, drained
- 1/4 cup chopped walnuts or pecans (optional)

For the Cream Cheese Glaze:

- 4 oz cream cheese, softened
- 1 cup powdered sugar
- 1 teaspoon vanilla extract
- 2-3 tablespoons milk

Instructions:

For the Donuts:

Preheat your oven to 350°F (175°C). Grease a donut pan.
In a large bowl, whisk together the flour, sugar, baking powder, baking soda, salt, cinnamon, and nutmeg.
In another bowl, whisk together the vegetable oil and egg until well combined.
Add the wet ingredients to the dry ingredients and stir until just combined. Do not overmix.
Fold in the grated carrot, crushed pineapple, and chopped nuts if using.
Spoon the batter into a piping bag or a zip-top bag with the corner snipped off.
Pipe the batter into the prepared donut pan, filling each cavity about 2/3 full.

Bake for 10-12 minutes or until the donuts are firm and a toothpick inserted into the center comes out clean.

Allow the donuts to cool in the pan for a few minutes before transferring them to a wire rack to cool completely.

For the Cream Cheese Glaze:

In a bowl, beat the softened cream cheese until smooth.

Add the powdered sugar and vanilla extract, and continue to beat until well combined.

Add milk, one tablespoon at a time, until you achieve a smooth and pourable consistency.

Assembly:

Dip the tops of each cooled donut into the cream cheese glaze, ensuring they are well coated.

Place the glazed donuts on a wire rack to allow excess glaze to drip off.

Allow the glaze to set for a few minutes before serving.

Enjoy your Carrot Cake Donuts with the classic flavors of carrot, pineapple, and cream cheese!

These donuts capture the essence of carrot cake in a delightful baked form, perfect for breakfast or as a sweet treat. The cream cheese glaze adds a decadent finishing touch.

Dulce de Leche Donuts

Ingredients:

For the Donuts:

- 1 1/2 cups all-purpose flour
- 1/2 cup granulated sugar
- 1 1/2 teaspoons baking powder
- 1/4 teaspoon baking soda
- 1/4 teaspoon salt
- 1/2 cup buttermilk
- 1/4 cup unsalted butter, melted
- 1 large egg
- 1 teaspoon vanilla extract
- 1/4 cup dulce de leche

For the Dulce de Leche Glaze:

- 1/2 cup dulce de leche
- 1 cup powdered sugar
- 2-3 tablespoons milk (adjust to achieve desired consistency)

Instructions:

For the Donuts:

Preheat your oven to 350°F (175°C). Grease a donut pan.
In a large bowl, whisk together the flour, sugar, baking powder, baking soda, and salt.
In another bowl, mix together the buttermilk, melted butter, egg, vanilla extract, and dulce de leche.
Add the wet ingredients to the dry ingredients and stir until just combined. Do not overmix.
Spoon the batter into a piping bag or a zip-top bag with the corner snipped off.
Pipe the batter into the prepared donut pan, filling each cavity about 2/3 full.
Bake for 10-12 minutes or until the donuts are firm and a toothpick inserted into the center comes out clean.
Allow the donuts to cool in the pan for a few minutes before transferring them to a wire rack to cool completely.

For the Dulce de Leche Glaze:

> In a heatproof bowl, warm the dulce de leche in the microwave or on the stove until it becomes smooth and pourable.
> Whisk together the powdered sugar, warm dulce de leche, and milk until you achieve a smooth glaze.

Assembly:

> Dip the tops of each cooled donut into the dulce de leche glaze, ensuring they are well coated.
> Place the glazed donuts on a wire rack to allow excess glaze to drip off.
> Allow the glaze to set for a few minutes before serving.
> Enjoy your Dulce de Leche Donuts with the rich and caramelized flavor of dulce de leche!

These donuts are a delightful way to enjoy the sweet and creamy taste of dulce de leche. Perfect for breakfast or as a special treat with a cup of coffee.

Honey Glazed Donuts

Ingredients:

For the Donuts:

- 2 cups all-purpose flour
- 1/2 cup granulated sugar
- 1 1/2 teaspoons baking powder
- 1/4 teaspoon baking soda
- 1/2 teaspoon salt
- 1/2 cup buttermilk
- 1/4 cup unsalted butter, melted
- 2 large eggs
- 1 teaspoon vanilla extract

For the Honey Glaze:

- 1/4 cup unsalted butter
- 1/4 cup honey
- 1/2 cup powdered sugar
- 1/2 teaspoon vanilla extract

Instructions:

For the Donuts:

> Preheat your oven to 350°F (175°C). Grease a donut pan.
> In a large bowl, whisk together the flour, sugar, baking powder, baking soda, and salt.
> In another bowl, mix together the buttermilk, melted butter, eggs, and vanilla extract.
> Add the wet ingredients to the dry ingredients and stir until just combined. Do not overmix.
> Spoon the batter into a piping bag or a zip-top bag with the corner snipped off.
> Pipe the batter into the prepared donut pan, filling each cavity about 2/3 full.
> Bake for 10-12 minutes or until the donuts are firm and a toothpick inserted into the center comes out clean.
> Allow the donuts to cool in the pan for a few minutes before transferring them to a wire rack to cool completely.

For the Honey Glaze:

- In a small saucepan over low heat, melt the butter.
- Stir in the honey until well combined.
- Remove the saucepan from heat and whisk in the powdered sugar and vanilla extract until smooth.

Assembly:

- Dip the tops of each cooled donut into the honey glaze, ensuring they are well coated.
- Place the glazed donuts on a wire rack to allow excess glaze to drip off.
- Allow the glaze to set for a few minutes before serving.
- Enjoy your Honey Glazed Donuts with the sweet and sticky goodness of honey!

These donuts are a simple yet delightful treat, perfect for breakfast or as an afternoon snack. The honey glaze adds a natural sweetness that complements the soft and fluffy donuts.

Pistachio Cherry Donuts

Ingredients:

For the Donuts:

- 1 1/2 cups all-purpose flour
- 1/2 cup granulated sugar
- 1 1/2 teaspoons baking powder
- 1/4 teaspoon baking soda
- 1/4 teaspoon salt
- 1/2 cup buttermilk
- 1/4 cup unsalted butter, melted
- 1/2 cup shelled pistachios, finely ground
- 1/2 cup chopped fresh cherries (pitted)

For the Pistachio Cherry Glaze:

- 1 cup powdered sugar
- 2 tablespoons pistachio paste (you can make this by blending shelled pistachios until smooth)
- 2 tablespoons cherry juice (from the chopped cherries)
- Chopped pistachios and sliced cherries for topping (optional)

Instructions:

For the Donuts:

Preheat your oven to 350°F (175°C). Grease a donut pan.
In a large bowl, whisk together the flour, sugar, baking powder, baking soda, and salt.
In another bowl, mix together the buttermilk, melted butter, ground pistachios, and chopped cherries.
Add the wet ingredients to the dry ingredients and stir until just combined. Do not overmix.
Spoon the batter into a piping bag or a zip-top bag with the corner snipped off.
Pipe the batter into the prepared donut pan, filling each cavity about 2/3 full.
Bake for 10-12 minutes or until the donuts are firm and a toothpick inserted into the center comes out clean.

Allow the donuts to cool in the pan for a few minutes before transferring them to a wire rack to cool completely.

For the Pistachio Cherry Glaze:

In a bowl, whisk together the powdered sugar, pistachio paste, and cherry juice until smooth.

Assembly:

Dip the tops of each cooled donut into the pistachio cherry glaze, ensuring they are well coated.
Place the glazed donuts on a wire rack to allow excess glaze to drip off.
Optionally, sprinkle chopped pistachios and place sliced cherries on top of the glazed donuts.
Allow the glaze to set for a few minutes before serving.
Enjoy your Pistachio Cherry Donuts with the delightful combination of nutty pistachios and sweet cherries!

These donuts offer a unique and flavorful twist, making them a perfect choice for a special breakfast or dessert. The pistachio and cherry combination creates a wonderful balance of taste and texture.

Pineapple Upside-Down Donuts

Ingredients:

For the Pineapple Topping:

- 1/4 cup unsalted butter
- 1/2 cup brown sugar, packed
- 1 can (20 ounces) pineapple slices, drained
- Maraschino cherries for topping

For the Donuts:

- 1 1/2 cups all-purpose flour
- 1/2 cup granulated sugar
- 1 1/2 teaspoons baking powder
- 1/4 teaspoon baking soda
- 1/4 teaspoon salt
- 1/2 cup buttermilk
- 1/4 cup unsalted butter, melted
- 1/4 cup pineapple juice (reserved from the canned pineapple)
- 1 large egg
- 1 teaspoon vanilla extract

Instructions:

For the Pineapple Topping:

Preheat your oven to 350°F (175°C). Grease a donut pan.
In a small saucepan, melt the butter over medium heat. Add brown sugar and stir until well combined and melted.
Spoon the brown sugar mixture into the bottom of each donut cavity, ensuring an even distribution.
Place a pineapple slice on top of the brown sugar mixture in each donut cavity.
Add a maraschino cherry in the center of each pineapple ring.

For the Donuts:

In a large bowl, whisk together the flour, sugar, baking powder, baking soda, and salt.

In another bowl, mix together the buttermilk, melted butter, pineapple juice, egg, and vanilla extract.

Add the wet ingredients to the dry ingredients and stir until just combined. Do not overmix.

Spoon the batter into a piping bag or a zip-top bag with the corner snipped off.

Pipe the batter over the pineapple slices in the donut cavities, filling each about 2/3 full.

Bake for 10-12 minutes or until the donuts are firm and a toothpick inserted into the center comes out clean.

Allow the donuts to cool in the pan for a few minutes before transferring them to a wire rack to cool completely.

Assembly:

Once cooled, gently invert the donut pan onto a serving platter, allowing the pineapple slices to become the topping of each donut.

If any pineapple slices stick to the pan, carefully remove and place them back onto the donuts.

Serve your Pineapple Upside-Down Donuts and enjoy this delightful twist on a classic dessert!

These donuts offer the tropical flavors of pineapple upside-down cake in a convenient and adorable donut form. Perfect for a sweet breakfast treat or a unique dessert!

Cranberry Orange Donuts

Ingredients:

For the Donuts:

- 1 1/2 cups all-purpose flour
- 1/2 cup granulated sugar
- 1 1/2 teaspoons baking powder
- 1/4 teaspoon baking soda
- 1/4 teaspoon salt
- 1/2 cup buttermilk
- 1/4 cup unsalted butter, melted
- Zest of 1 orange
- 1/4 cup fresh orange juice
- 1 large egg
- 1 teaspoon vanilla extract
- 1/2 cup fresh or frozen cranberries, chopped

For the Orange Glaze:

- 1 cup powdered sugar
- 2 tablespoons fresh orange juice
- Zest of 1 orange

Instructions:

For the Donuts:

Preheat your oven to 350°F (175°C). Grease a donut pan.
In a large bowl, whisk together the flour, sugar, baking powder, baking soda, and salt.
In another bowl, mix together the buttermilk, melted butter, orange zest, orange juice, egg, and vanilla extract.
Add the wet ingredients to the dry ingredients and stir until just combined. Do not overmix.
Gently fold in the chopped cranberries.
Spoon the batter into a piping bag or a zip-top bag with the corner snipped off.
Pipe the batter into the prepared donut pan, filling each cavity about 2/3 full.

Bake for 10-12 minutes or until the donuts are firm and a toothpick inserted into the center comes out clean.
Allow the donuts to cool in the pan for a few minutes before transferring them to a wire rack to cool completely.

For the Orange Glaze:

In a bowl, whisk together the powdered sugar, fresh orange juice, and orange zest until smooth.

Assembly:

Dip the tops of each cooled donut into the orange glaze, ensuring they are well coated.
Place the glazed donuts on a wire rack to allow excess glaze to drip off.
Allow the glaze to set for a few minutes before serving.
Enjoy your Cranberry Orange Donuts with the perfect combination of tart cranberries and zesty orange!

These donuts are a burst of flavor, combining the tartness of cranberries with the citrusy notes of orange. A delightful treat for breakfast or a sweet snack!

White Chocolate Raspberry Donuts

Ingredients:

For the Donuts:

- 1 1/2 cups all-purpose flour
- 1/2 cup granulated sugar
- 1 1/2 teaspoons baking powder
- 1/4 teaspoon baking soda
- 1/4 teaspoon salt
- 1/2 cup buttermilk
- 1/4 cup unsalted butter, melted
- 1/2 cup fresh raspberries, mashed
- 1 large egg
- 1 teaspoon vanilla extract
- 1/2 cup white chocolate chips

For the White Chocolate Glaze:

- 1/2 cup white chocolate chips
- 2 tablespoons heavy cream
- 1/2 teaspoon vanilla extract

Additional fresh raspberries for topping (optional)

Instructions:

For the Donuts:

Preheat your oven to 350°F (175°C). Grease a donut pan.
In a large bowl, whisk together the flour, sugar, baking powder, baking soda, and salt.
In another bowl, mix together the buttermilk, melted butter, mashed raspberries, egg, and vanilla extract.

Add the wet ingredients to the dry ingredients and stir until just combined. Do not overmix.

Fold in the white chocolate chips.

Spoon the batter into a piping bag or a zip-top bag with the corner snipped off.

Pipe the batter into the prepared donut pan, filling each cavity about 2/3 full.

Bake for 10-12 minutes or until the donuts are firm and a toothpick inserted into the center comes out clean.

Allow the donuts to cool in the pan for a few minutes before transferring them to a wire rack to cool completely.

For the White Chocolate Glaze:

In a heatproof bowl, melt the white chocolate chips and heavy cream together, either in a microwave or using a double boiler, stirring until smooth.

Stir in the vanilla extract.

Assembly:

Dip the tops of each cooled donut into the white chocolate glaze, ensuring they are well coated.

Optionally, top each glazed donut with additional fresh raspberries for added freshness and flavor.

Allow the glaze to set for a few minutes before serving.

Enjoy your White Chocolate Raspberry Donuts with the perfect combination of sweet white chocolate and tart raspberries!

These donuts offer a delightful contrast of flavors, making them a perfect choice for a special breakfast or dessert. The white chocolate and raspberry pairing creates a deliciously sweet and fruity treat.

Raspberry Almond Donuts

Ingredients:

For the Donuts:

- 1 1/2 cups all-purpose flour
- 1/2 cup granulated sugar
- 1 1/2 teaspoons baking powder
- 1/4 teaspoon baking soda
- 1/4 teaspoon salt
- 1/2 cup buttermilk
- 1/4 cup unsalted butter, melted
- 1/2 cup fresh raspberries, mashed
- 1 large egg
- 1 teaspoon almond extract
- 1/4 cup sliced almonds

For the Almond Glaze:

- 1 cup powdered sugar
- 2 tablespoons milk
- 1/2 teaspoon almond extract
- Sliced almonds for topping (optional)

Instructions:

For the Donuts:

Preheat your oven to 350°F (175°C). Grease a donut pan.
In a large bowl, whisk together the flour, sugar, baking powder, baking soda, and salt.
In another bowl, mix together the buttermilk, melted butter, mashed raspberries, egg, and almond extract.
Add the wet ingredients to the dry ingredients and stir until just combined. Do not overmix.
Gently fold in the sliced almonds.

Spoon the batter into a piping bag or a zip-top bag with the corner snipped off. Pipe the batter into the prepared donut pan, filling each cavity about 2/3 full.
Bake for 10-12 minutes or until the donuts are firm and a toothpick inserted into the center comes out clean.
Allow the donuts to cool in the pan for a few minutes before transferring them to a wire rack to cool completely.

For the Almond Glaze:

In a bowl, whisk together the powdered sugar, milk, and almond extract until smooth.

Assembly:

Dip the tops of each cooled donut into the almond glaze, ensuring they are well coated.
Optionally, top each glazed donut with additional sliced almonds for added crunch.
Allow the glaze to set for a few minutes before serving.
Enjoy your Raspberry Almond Donuts with the perfect combination of fruity raspberries and nutty almonds!

These donuts offer a delightful blend of flavors and textures, making them a perfect choice for breakfast or a sweet treat. The almond extract enhances the nutty flavor, complementing the brightness of the raspberries.

Irish Cream Glazed Donuts

Ingredients:

For the Donuts:

- 1 1/2 cups all-purpose flour
- 1/2 cup granulated sugar
- 1 1/2 teaspoons baking powder
- 1/4 teaspoon baking soda
- 1/4 teaspoon salt
- 1/2 cup buttermilk
- 1/4 cup unsalted butter, melted
- 1/4 cup Irish cream liqueur (e.g., Baileys)
- 1 large egg
- 1 teaspoon vanilla extract

For the Irish Cream Glaze:

- 1 cup powdered sugar
- 2 tablespoons Irish cream liqueur
- 1/2 teaspoon vanilla extract

Instructions:

For the Donuts:

Preheat your oven to 350°F (175°C). Grease a donut pan.
In a large bowl, whisk together the flour, sugar, baking powder, baking soda, and salt.
In another bowl, mix together the buttermilk, melted butter, Irish cream liqueur, egg, and vanilla extract.
Add the wet ingredients to the dry ingredients and stir until just combined. Do not overmix.
Spoon the batter into a piping bag or a zip-top bag with the corner snipped off.
Pipe the batter into the prepared donut pan, filling each cavity about 2/3 full.
Bake for 10-12 minutes or until the donuts are firm and a toothpick inserted into the center comes out clean.
Allow the donuts to cool in the pan for a few minutes before transferring them to a wire rack to cool completely.

For the Irish Cream Glaze:

In a bowl, whisk together the powdered sugar, Irish cream liqueur, and vanilla extract until smooth.

Assembly:

Dip the tops of each cooled donut into the Irish Cream glaze, ensuring they are well coated.
Place the glazed donuts on a wire rack to allow excess glaze to drip off.
Allow the glaze to set for a few minutes before serving.
Enjoy your Irish Cream Glazed Donuts with the rich and creamy flavor of Irish cream!

These donuts offer a delightful twist with the addition of Irish cream, making them perfect for a special breakfast or dessert. The glaze adds a luxurious touch, making each bite a heavenly experience.

Banana Nut Donuts

Ingredients:

For the Donuts:

- 1 1/2 cups all-purpose flour
- 1/2 cup granulated sugar
- 1 1/2 teaspoons baking powder
- 1/4 teaspoon baking soda
- 1/4 teaspoon salt
- 3 ripe bananas, mashed
- 1/4 cup unsalted butter, melted
- 1/4 cup buttermilk
- 1 large egg
- 1 teaspoon vanilla extract
- 1/2 cup chopped walnuts or pecans

For the Cream Cheese Frosting:

- 4 oz cream cheese, softened
- 1/2 cup powdered sugar
- 1/2 teaspoon vanilla extract
- Chopped nuts for topping (optional)

Instructions:

For the Donuts:

Preheat your oven to 350°F (175°C). Grease a donut pan.
In a large bowl, whisk together the flour, sugar, baking powder, baking soda, and salt.
In another bowl, mix together the mashed bananas, melted butter, buttermilk, egg, and vanilla extract.
Add the wet ingredients to the dry ingredients and stir until just combined. Do not overmix.
Fold in the chopped nuts.

Spoon the batter into a piping bag or a zip-top bag with the corner snipped off.
Pipe the batter into the prepared donut pan, filling each cavity about 2/3 full.
Bake for 10-12 minutes or until the donuts are firm and a toothpick inserted into the center comes out clean.
Allow the donuts to cool in the pan for a few minutes before transferring them to a wire rack to cool completely.

For the Cream Cheese Frosting:

In a bowl, beat the softened cream cheese until smooth.
Add the powdered sugar and vanilla extract, and continue to beat until well combined.

Assembly:

Once the donuts are completely cooled, spread or drizzle the cream cheese frosting over the tops of each donut.
Optionally, sprinkle chopped nuts on top for added texture and flavor.
Allow the frosting to set for a few minutes before serving.
Enjoy your Banana Nut Donuts with the delicious combination of banana sweetness and nutty crunch!

These donuts offer a comforting and flavorful experience, making them a perfect choice for breakfast or a delightful snack. The cream cheese frosting adds a creamy and tangy element, complementing the natural sweetness of the bananas.

Chocolate Peanut Butter Pretzel Donuts

Ingredients:

For the Donuts:

- 1 cup all-purpose flour
- 1/4 cup cocoa powder
- 1/2 cup granulated sugar
- 1 teaspoon baking powder
- 1/4 teaspoon baking soda
- 1/4 teaspoon salt
- 1/2 cup buttermilk
- 1/4 cup vegetable oil
- 1 large egg
- 1 teaspoon vanilla extract

For the Peanut Butter Glaze:

- 1/2 cup creamy peanut butter
- 1/2 cup powdered sugar
- 2-3 tablespoons milk

For the Pretzel Topping:

- 1/2 cup pretzels, crushed

Instructions:

For the Donuts:

> Preheat your oven to 350°F (175°C). Grease a donut pan.
> In a large bowl, whisk together the flour, cocoa powder, sugar, baking powder, baking soda, and salt.
> In another bowl, mix together the buttermilk, vegetable oil, egg, and vanilla extract.
> Add the wet ingredients to the dry ingredients and stir until just combined. Do not overmix.
> Spoon the batter into a piping bag or a zip-top bag with the corner snipped off.
> Pipe the batter into the prepared donut pan, filling each cavity about 2/3 full.

Bake for 10-12 minutes or until the donuts are firm and a toothpick inserted into the center comes out clean.

Allow the donuts to cool in the pan for a few minutes before transferring them to a wire rack to cool completely.

For the Peanut Butter Glaze:

In a bowl, whisk together the peanut butter, powdered sugar, and milk until smooth.

Assembly:

Once the donuts are completely cooled, dip the tops of each donut into the peanut butter glaze, ensuring they are well coated.

Place the glazed donuts on a wire rack to allow excess glaze to drip off.

Immediately sprinkle the crushed pretzels over the peanut butter glaze before it sets.

Allow the glaze to set for a few minutes before serving.

Enjoy your Chocolate Peanut Butter Pretzel Donuts with the perfect balance of chocolate, peanut butter, and crunchy pretzels!

These donuts offer a delightful mix of sweet and salty flavors, making them an indulgent treat for breakfast or dessert. The combination of chocolate, peanut butter, and pretzels creates a satisfying and delicious experience.

Vanilla Bean Glazed Donuts

Ingredients:

For the Donuts:

- 1 1/2 cups all-purpose flour
- 1/2 cup granulated sugar
- 1 1/2 teaspoons baking powder
- 1/4 teaspoon baking soda
- 1/4 teaspoon salt
- 1/2 cup buttermilk
- 1/4 cup unsalted butter, melted
- 1 large egg
- 1 teaspoon vanilla extract
- Seeds scraped from 1 vanilla bean (or 1 additional teaspoon of vanilla extract)

For the Vanilla Bean Glaze:

- 1 cup powdered sugar
- Seeds scraped from 1 vanilla bean (or 1 teaspoon vanilla bean paste)
- 2-3 tablespoons milk

Instructions:

For the Donuts:

Preheat your oven to 350°F (175°C). Grease a donut pan.
In a large bowl, whisk together the flour, sugar, baking powder, baking soda, and salt.
In another bowl, mix together the buttermilk, melted butter, egg, vanilla extract, and scraped vanilla bean seeds.
Add the wet ingredients to the dry ingredients and stir until just combined. Do not overmix.
Spoon the batter into a piping bag or a zip-top bag with the corner snipped off.
Pipe the batter into the prepared donut pan, filling each cavity about 2/3 full.

Bake for 10-12 minutes or until the donuts are firm and a toothpick inserted into the center comes out clean.

Allow the donuts to cool in the pan for a few minutes before transferring them to a wire rack to cool completely.

For the Vanilla Bean Glaze:

In a bowl, whisk together the powdered sugar, scraped vanilla bean seeds, and milk until smooth.

Assembly:

Dip the tops of each cooled donut into the vanilla bean glaze, ensuring they are well coated.

Place the glazed donuts on a wire rack to allow excess glaze to drip off.

Allow the glaze to set for a few minutes before serving.

Enjoy your Vanilla Bean Glazed Donuts with the exquisite flavor of real vanilla beans!

These donuts offer a sophisticated twist with the addition of real vanilla bean seeds, creating a rich and aromatic experience. Perfect for a special breakfast or a delightful treat any time of day.

Triple Chocolate Donuts

Ingredients:

For the Donuts:

- 1 cup all-purpose flour
- 1/4 cup cocoa powder
- 1/2 cup granulated sugar
- 1 teaspoon baking powder
- 1/4 teaspoon baking soda
- 1/4 teaspoon salt
- 1/2 cup buttermilk
- 1/4 cup vegetable oil
- 1 large egg
- 1 teaspoon vanilla extract
- 1/2 cup chocolate chips

For the Chocolate Glaze:

- 1/2 cup semi-sweet chocolate chips
- 3 tablespoons unsalted butter
- 1 tablespoon corn syrup or honey
- 1/2 teaspoon vanilla extract

Instructions:

For the Donuts:

> Preheat your oven to 350°F (175°C). Grease a donut pan.
> In a large bowl, whisk together the flour, cocoa powder, sugar, baking powder, baking soda, and salt.
> In another bowl, mix together the buttermilk, vegetable oil, egg, and vanilla extract.
> Add the wet ingredients to the dry ingredients and stir until just combined. Do not overmix.
> Fold in the chocolate chips.
> Spoon the batter into a piping bag or a zip-top bag with the corner snipped off.
> Pipe the batter into the prepared donut pan, filling each cavity about 2/3 full.

Bake for 10-12 minutes or until the donuts are firm and a toothpick inserted into the center comes out clean.

Allow the donuts to cool in the pan for a few minutes before transferring them to a wire rack to cool completely.

For the Chocolate Glaze:

In a heatproof bowl, melt the chocolate chips, butter, and corn syrup (or honey) together. You can do this in a microwave or using a double boiler, stirring until smooth.

Stir in the vanilla extract.

Assembly:

Dip the tops of each cooled donut into the chocolate glaze, ensuring they are well coated.

Place the glazed donuts on a wire rack to allow excess glaze to drip off.

Allow the glaze to set for a few minutes before serving.

Enjoy your Triple Chocolate Donuts with an abundance of chocolatey goodness!

These donuts are a true delight for chocolate lovers, with the triple combination of cocoa, chocolate chips, and a rich chocolate glaze. Perfect for a sweet breakfast or a decadent dessert.

Key Lime Pie Donuts

Ingredients:

For the Donuts:

- 1 1/2 cups all-purpose flour
- 1/2 cup granulated sugar
- 1 1/2 teaspoons baking powder
- 1/4 teaspoon baking soda
- 1/4 teaspoon salt
- 1/2 cup buttermilk
- 1/4 cup vegetable oil
- 1 large egg
- Zest of 2 key limes
- 2 tablespoons key lime juice
- 1 teaspoon vanilla extract

For the Key Lime Glaze:

- 1 cup powdered sugar
- 2 tablespoons key lime juice
- Additional key lime zest for topping

Instructions:

For the Donuts:

Preheat your oven to 350°F (175°C). Grease a donut pan.
In a large bowl, whisk together the flour, sugar, baking powder, baking soda, and salt.
In another bowl, mix together the buttermilk, vegetable oil, egg, key lime zest, key lime juice, and vanilla extract.
Add the wet ingredients to the dry ingredients and stir until just combined. Do not overmix.
Spoon the batter into a piping bag or a zip-top bag with the corner snipped off.
Pipe the batter into the prepared donut pan, filling each cavity about 2/3 full.

Bake for 10-12 minutes or until the donuts are firm and a toothpick inserted into the center comes out clean.

Allow the donuts to cool in the pan for a few minutes before transferring them to a wire rack to cool completely.

For the Key Lime Glaze:

In a bowl, whisk together the powdered sugar and key lime juice until smooth.

Assembly:

Dip the tops of each cooled donut into the key lime glaze, ensuring they are well coated.

Place the glazed donuts on a wire rack to allow excess glaze to drip off.

Immediately sprinkle additional key lime zest over the glaze before it sets.

Allow the glaze to set for a few minutes before serving.

Enjoy your Key Lime Pie Donuts with the vibrant and citrusy flavors of key lime!

These donuts offer a taste of the tropics with the zesty essence of key lime pie. Perfect for a refreshing breakfast or a sweet snack.

Rum Raisin Donuts

Ingredients:

For the Donuts:

- 1 cup raisins
- 1/4 cup dark rum
- 1 1/2 cups all-purpose flour
- 1/2 cup granulated sugar
- 1 1/2 teaspoons baking powder
- 1/4 teaspoon baking soda
- 1/4 teaspoon salt
- 1/2 cup buttermilk
- 1/4 cup unsalted butter, melted
- 1 large egg
- 1 teaspoon vanilla extract
- 1/2 cup chopped nuts (walnuts or pecans), optional

For the Rum Glaze:

- 1 cup powdered sugar
- 2 tablespoons dark rum
- 1/2 teaspoon vanilla extract

Instructions:

For the Rum-Soaked Raisins:

In a small bowl, combine the raisins and dark rum. Allow them to soak for at least 30 minutes or until the raisins are plump and have absorbed the rum.

For the Donuts:

Preheat your oven to 350°F (175°C). Grease a donut pan.
In a large bowl, whisk together the flour, sugar, baking powder, baking soda, and salt.
In another bowl, mix together the buttermilk, melted butter, egg, vanilla extract, and the rum-soaked raisins (including any remaining rum).

Add the wet ingredients to the dry ingredients and stir until just combined. Do not overmix.

If desired, fold in the chopped nuts.

Spoon the batter into a piping bag or a zip-top bag with the corner snipped off.

Pipe the batter into the prepared donut pan, filling each cavity about 2/3 full.

Bake for 10-12 minutes or until the donuts are firm and a toothpick inserted into the center comes out clean.

Allow the donuts to cool in the pan for a few minutes before transferring them to a wire rack to cool completely.

For the Rum Glaze:

In a bowl, whisk together the powdered sugar, dark rum, and vanilla extract until smooth.

Assembly:

Dip the tops of each cooled donut into the rum glaze, ensuring they are well coated.

Place the glazed donuts on a wire rack to allow excess glaze to drip off.

Allow the glaze to set for a few minutes before serving.

Enjoy your Rum Raisin Donuts with the delightful combination of rum-soaked raisins and a flavorful glaze!

These donuts offer a warm and comforting flavor profile, perfect for a special breakfast or a sweet treat. The rum-soaked raisins add a rich and aromatic element to the overall experience.

Pistachio Rosewater Donuts

Ingredients:

For the Donuts:

- 1 1/2 cups all-purpose flour
- 1/2 cup granulated sugar
- 1 1/2 teaspoons baking powder
- 1/4 teaspoon baking soda
- 1/4 teaspoon salt
- 1/2 cup buttermilk
- 1/4 cup unsalted butter, melted
- 1/4 cup shelled pistachios, finely ground
- 1 large egg
- 1 teaspoon rosewater
- Chopped pistachios for topping

For the Rosewater Glaze:

- 1 cup powdered sugar
- 1-2 tablespoons milk
- 1/2 teaspoon rosewater

Instructions:

For the Donuts:

Preheat your oven to 350°F (175°C). Grease a donut pan.
In a food processor, grind the shelled pistachios until finely ground. Be careful not to over-process into a paste; you want a crumbly texture.
In a large bowl, whisk together the flour, sugar, baking powder, baking soda, and salt.
In another bowl, mix together the buttermilk, melted butter, ground pistachios, egg, and rosewater.
Add the wet ingredients to the dry ingredients and stir until just combined. Do not overmix.
Spoon the batter into a piping bag or a zip-top bag with the corner snipped off.
Pipe the batter into the prepared donut pan, filling each cavity about 2/3 full.

Bake for 10-12 minutes or until the donuts are firm and a toothpick inserted into the center comes out clean.
Allow the donuts to cool in the pan for a few minutes before transferring them to a wire rack to cool completely.

For the Rosewater Glaze:

In a bowl, whisk together the powdered sugar, 1 tablespoon of milk, and rosewater. Add more milk if needed to reach your desired glaze consistency.

Assembly:

Dip the tops of each cooled donut into the rosewater glaze, ensuring they are well coated.
Sprinkle chopped pistachios on top of the glazed donuts.
Place the glazed donuts on a wire rack to allow excess glaze to drip off.
Allow the glaze to set for a few minutes before serving.
Enjoy your Pistachio Rosewater Donuts with the unique combination of nutty pistachios and floral rosewater!

These donuts offer an elegant and exotic flavor profile, making them a perfect choice for a special breakfast or a delightful dessert. The combination of pistachios and rosewater creates a fragrant and delicious treat.

Caramel Apple Donuts

Ingredients:

For the Donuts:

- 1 1/2 cups all-purpose flour
- 1/2 cup granulated sugar
- 1 1/2 teaspoons baking powder
- 1/4 teaspoon baking soda
- 1/4 teaspoon salt
- 1/2 cup buttermilk
- 1/4 cup unsalted butter, melted
- 1 large egg
- 1 teaspoon vanilla extract
- 1 cup finely diced apples (peeled and cored)

For the Caramel Glaze:

- 1/2 cup unsalted butter
- 1 cup brown sugar
- 1/4 cup heavy cream
- 1/2 teaspoon vanilla extract
- Pinch of salt

Instructions:

For the Donuts:

Preheat your oven to 350°F (175°C). Grease a donut pan.
In a large bowl, whisk together the flour, sugar, baking powder, baking soda, and salt.
In another bowl, mix together the buttermilk, melted butter, egg, and vanilla extract.
Add the wet ingredients to the dry ingredients and stir until just combined. Do not overmix.
Gently fold in the diced apples.

Spoon the batter into a piping bag or a zip-top bag with the corner snipped off.
Pipe the batter into the prepared donut pan, filling each cavity about 2/3 full.
Bake for 10-12 minutes or until the donuts are firm and a toothpick inserted into the center comes out clean.
Allow the donuts to cool in the pan for a few minutes before transferring them to a wire rack to cool completely.

For the Caramel Glaze:

In a saucepan over medium heat, melt the butter.
Stir in the brown sugar and cook until it dissolves, stirring constantly.
Add the heavy cream, vanilla extract, and a pinch of salt. Bring the mixture to a simmer and cook for 2-3 minutes until the caramel thickens.
Remove the caramel from heat and let it cool slightly.

Assembly:

Dip the tops of each cooled donut into the caramel glaze, ensuring they are well coated.
Place the glazed donuts on a wire rack to allow excess glaze to drip off.
Allow the glaze to set for a few minutes before serving.
Enjoy your Caramel Apple Donuts with the perfect combination of sweet caramel and tart apples!

These donuts offer a delightful taste of fall with the classic pairing of caramel and apples. Perfect for breakfast or a sweet treat any time of the year.

Lavender Honey Donuts

Ingredients:

For the Donuts:

- 1 1/2 cups all-purpose flour
- 1/2 cup granulated sugar
- 1 1/2 teaspoons baking powder
- 1/4 teaspoon baking soda
- 1/4 teaspoon salt
- 1/2 cup buttermilk
- 1/4 cup unsalted butter, melted
- 1 large egg
- 1 teaspoon vanilla extract
- 1 tablespoon dried culinary lavender buds, finely ground

For the Honey Glaze:

- 1/2 cup powdered sugar
- 2 tablespoons honey
- 1-2 tablespoons milk
- Lavender buds for garnish (optional)

Instructions:

For the Donuts:

Preheat your oven to 350°F (175°C). Grease a donut pan.
In a spice grinder or mortar and pestle, finely grind the dried lavender buds.
In a large bowl, whisk together the flour, sugar, baking powder, baking soda, and salt.
In another bowl, mix together the buttermilk, melted butter, egg, vanilla extract, and ground lavender.
Add the wet ingredients to the dry ingredients and stir until just combined. Do not overmix.

Spoon the batter into a piping bag or a zip-top bag with the corner snipped off.
Pipe the batter into the prepared donut pan, filling each cavity about 2/3 full.
Bake for 10-12 minutes or until the donuts are firm and a toothpick inserted into the center comes out clean.
Allow the donuts to cool in the pan for a few minutes before transferring them to a wire rack to cool completely.

For the Honey Glaze:

In a bowl, whisk together the powdered sugar, honey, and 1 tablespoon of milk.
Add more milk if needed to reach your desired glaze consistency.

Assembly:

Dip the tops of each cooled donut into the honey glaze, ensuring they are well coated.
Place the glazed donuts on a wire rack to allow excess glaze to drip off.
Optionally, sprinkle additional lavender buds on top for a decorative touch.
Allow the glaze to set for a few minutes before serving.
Enjoy your Lavender Honey Donuts with the delightful combination of floral lavender and sweet honey!

These donuts offer a unique and sophisticated flavor profile, making them a perfect choice for a special breakfast or a delightful dessert. The lavender adds a subtle floral note, complementing the sweetness of the honey.

Pomegranate Blueberry Donuts

Ingredients:

For the Donuts:

- 1 1/2 cups all-purpose flour
- 1/2 cup granulated sugar
- 1 1/2 teaspoons baking powder
- 1/4 teaspoon baking soda
- 1/4 teaspoon salt
- 1/2 cup buttermilk
- 1/4 cup vegetable oil
- 1 large egg
- 1 teaspoon vanilla extract
- 1/2 cup fresh blueberries

For the Pomegranate Glaze:

- 1 cup powdered sugar
- 2 tablespoons pomegranate juice
- Pomegranate arils for topping (optional)

Instructions:

For the Donuts:

Preheat your oven to 350°F (175°C). Grease a donut pan.
In a large bowl, whisk together the flour, sugar, baking powder, baking soda, and salt.
In another bowl, mix together the buttermilk, vegetable oil, egg, and vanilla extract.
Add the wet ingredients to the dry ingredients and stir until just combined. Do not overmix.
Gently fold in the fresh blueberries.
Spoon the batter into a piping bag or a zip-top bag with the corner snipped off.
Pipe the batter into the prepared donut pan, filling each cavity about 2/3 full.

Bake for 10-12 minutes or until the donuts are firm and a toothpick inserted into the center comes out clean.
Allow the donuts to cool in the pan for a few minutes before transferring them to a wire rack to cool completely.

For the Pomegranate Glaze:

In a bowl, whisk together the powdered sugar and pomegranate juice until smooth.

Assembly:

Dip the tops of each cooled donut into the pomegranate glaze, ensuring they are well coated.
Place the glazed donuts on a wire rack to allow excess glaze to drip off.
Optionally, top each glazed donut with pomegranate arils for a burst of freshness and color.
Allow the glaze to set for a few minutes before serving.
Enjoy your Pomegranate Blueberry Donuts with the delightful combination of juicy blueberries and tangy pomegranate!

These donuts offer a fruity and refreshing twist, making them a perfect choice for breakfast or a sweet treat. The combination of blueberries and pomegranate creates a burst of flavor in every bite.

Gingerbread Spiced Donuts

Ingredients:

For the Donuts:

- 1 1/2 cups all-purpose flour
- 1/2 cup brown sugar, packed
- 1 teaspoon baking powder
- 1/2 teaspoon baking soda
- 1/4 teaspoon salt
- 1 teaspoon ground ginger
- 1 teaspoon ground cinnamon
- 1/4 teaspoon ground nutmeg
- 1/4 teaspoon ground cloves
- 1/2 cup buttermilk
- 1/4 cup unsalted butter, melted
- 1/4 cup molasses
- 1 large egg
- 1 teaspoon vanilla extract

For the Cinnamon Sugar Coating:

- 1/4 cup granulated sugar
- 1 teaspoon ground cinnamon

Instructions:

For the Donuts:

Preheat your oven to 350°F (175°C). Grease a donut pan.
In a large bowl, whisk together the flour, brown sugar, baking powder, baking soda, salt, ground ginger, ground cinnamon, ground nutmeg, and ground cloves.
In another bowl, mix together the buttermilk, melted butter, molasses, egg, and vanilla extract.
Add the wet ingredients to the dry ingredients and stir until just combined. Do not overmix.

Spoon the batter into a piping bag or a zip-top bag with the corner snipped off. Pipe the batter into the prepared donut pan, filling each cavity about 2/3 full.
Bake for 10-12 minutes or until the donuts are firm and a toothpick inserted into the center comes out clean.
Allow the donuts to cool in the pan for a few minutes before transferring them to a wire rack to cool completely.

For the Cinnamon Sugar Coating:

In a shallow bowl, mix together the granulated sugar and ground cinnamon.

Assembly:

While the donuts are still warm, dip each one into the cinnamon sugar coating, ensuring they are well coated.
Place the coated donuts on a wire rack to allow excess coating to fall off.
Allow the coating to set for a few minutes before serving.
Enjoy your Gingerbread Spiced Donuts with the warm and comforting flavors of ginger, cinnamon, and molasses!

These donuts capture the essence of gingerbread cookies, making them a delightful treat for the holiday season or any cozy occasion. The cinnamon sugar coating adds a sweet and aromatic finish to these spiced delights.

Chocolate Cherry Cordial Donuts

Ingredients:

For the Donuts:

- 1 1/2 cups all-purpose flour
- 1/2 cup cocoa powder
- 1/2 cup granulated sugar
- 1 teaspoon baking powder
- 1/2 teaspoon baking soda
- 1/4 teaspoon salt
- 1 cup buttermilk
- 1/4 cup vegetable oil
- 1 large egg
- 1 teaspoon vanilla extract
- 1/2 cup chocolate chips
- 1/2 cup maraschino cherries, chopped

For the Cherry Glaze:

- 1 cup powdered sugar
- 2 tablespoons maraschino cherry juice
- 1/4 teaspoon almond extract

Instructions:

For the Donuts:

Preheat your oven to 350°F (175°C). Grease a donut pan.
In a large bowl, whisk together the flour, cocoa powder, sugar, baking powder, baking soda, and salt.
In another bowl, mix together the buttermilk, vegetable oil, egg, and vanilla extract.
Add the wet ingredients to the dry ingredients and stir until just combined. Do not overmix.
Fold in the chocolate chips and chopped maraschino cherries.

Spoon the batter into a piping bag or a zip-top bag with the corner snipped off. Pipe the batter into the prepared donut pan, filling each cavity about 2/3 full.

Bake for 10-12 minutes or until the donuts are firm and a toothpick inserted into the center comes out clean.

Allow the donuts to cool in the pan for a few minutes before transferring them to a wire rack to cool completely.

For the Cherry Glaze:

In a bowl, whisk together the powdered sugar, maraschino cherry juice, and almond extract until smooth.

Assembly:

Dip the tops of each cooled donut into the cherry glaze, ensuring they are well coated.

Place the glazed donuts on a wire rack to allow excess glaze to drip off.

Allow the glaze to set for a few minutes before serving.

Optionally, garnish with additional chopped maraschino cherries or chocolate shavings.

Enjoy your Chocolate Cherry Cordial Donuts with the perfect blend of chocolate and cherry flavors!

These donuts bring together the classic combination of chocolate and cherries, reminiscent of a delicious cordial. Perfect for a special breakfast treat or a delightful dessert.

Coconut Mango Donuts

Ingredients:

For the Donuts:

- 1 1/2 cups all-purpose flour
- 1/2 cup granulated sugar
- 1 1/2 teaspoons baking powder
- 1/4 teaspoon baking soda
- 1/4 teaspoon salt
- 1/2 cup buttermilk
- 1/4 cup coconut oil, melted
- 1 large egg
- 1 teaspoon vanilla extract
- 1/2 cup finely diced ripe mango

For the Coconut Glaze:

- 1 cup powdered sugar
- 2 tablespoons coconut milk
- 1/4 cup shredded coconut (toasted, if desired)

Instructions:

For the Donuts:

Preheat your oven to 350°F (175°C). Grease a donut pan.
In a large bowl, whisk together the flour, sugar, baking powder, baking soda, and salt.
In another bowl, mix together the buttermilk, melted coconut oil, egg, and vanilla extract.
Add the wet ingredients to the dry ingredients and stir until just combined. Do not overmix.
Gently fold in the finely diced mango.
Spoon the batter into a piping bag or a zip-top bag with the corner snipped off.
Pipe the batter into the prepared donut pan, filling each cavity about 2/3 full.

Bake for 10-12 minutes or until the donuts are firm and a toothpick inserted into the center comes out clean.

Allow the donuts to cool in the pan for a few minutes before transferring them to a wire rack to cool completely.

For the Coconut Glaze:

In a bowl, whisk together the powdered sugar and coconut milk until smooth.

Assembly:

Dip the tops of each cooled donut into the coconut glaze, ensuring they are well coated.

Immediately sprinkle shredded coconut on top of the glazed donuts.

Place the glazed donuts on a wire rack to allow excess glaze to drip off.

Allow the glaze to set for a few minutes before serving.

Enjoy your Coconut Mango Donuts with the perfect blend of tropical flavors!

These donuts offer a taste of the tropics with the sweet and fruity combination of coconut and mango. Perfect for a special breakfast treat or a delightful dessert.

Strawberry Basil Donuts

Ingredients:

For the Donuts:

- 1 1/2 cups all-purpose flour
- 1/2 cup granulated sugar
- 1 1/2 teaspoons baking powder
- 1/4 teaspoon baking soda
- 1/4 teaspoon salt
- 1/2 cup buttermilk
- 1/4 cup unsalted butter, melted
- 1 large egg
- 1 teaspoon vanilla extract
- 1/2 cup fresh strawberries, diced
- 2 tablespoons fresh basil, finely chopped

For the Strawberry Basil Glaze:

- 1 cup powdered sugar
- 2 tablespoons strawberry puree (blend fresh strawberries and strain)
- 1 teaspoon fresh basil, finely chopped

Instructions:

For the Donuts:

Preheat your oven to 350°F (175°C). Grease a donut pan.
In a large bowl, whisk together the flour, sugar, baking powder, baking soda, and salt.
In another bowl, mix together the buttermilk, melted butter, egg, and vanilla extract.
Add the wet ingredients to the dry ingredients and stir until just combined. Do not overmix.
Gently fold in the diced strawberries and chopped basil.

Spoon the batter into a piping bag or a zip-top bag with the corner snipped off. Pipe the batter into the prepared donut pan, filling each cavity about 2/3 full. Bake for 10-12 minutes or until the donuts are firm and a toothpick inserted into the center comes out clean.

Allow the donuts to cool in the pan for a few minutes before transferring them to a wire rack to cool completely.

For the Strawberry Basil Glaze:

In a bowl, whisk together the powdered sugar, strawberry puree, and chopped basil until smooth.

Assembly:

Dip the tops of each cooled donut into the strawberry basil glaze, ensuring they are well coated.
Place the glazed donuts on a wire rack to allow excess glaze to drip off.
Allow the glaze to set for a few minutes before serving.
Enjoy your Strawberry Basil Donuts with the delightful combination of sweet strawberries and aromatic basil!

These donuts offer a refreshing and unique flavor profile, making them a perfect choice for a special breakfast or a delightful dessert. The addition of fresh basil adds a surprising twist to the classic strawberry flavor.

Caramel Macchiato Donuts

Ingredients:

For the Donuts:

- 1 1/2 cups all-purpose flour
- 1/2 cup granulated sugar
- 1 1/2 teaspoons baking powder
- 1/4 teaspoon baking soda
- 1/4 teaspoon salt
- 1/2 cup buttermilk
- 1/4 cup strong brewed coffee, cooled
- 1/4 cup vegetable oil
- 1 large egg
- 1 teaspoon vanilla extract

For the Caramel Glaze:

- 1/2 cup unsalted butter
- 1 cup brown sugar, packed
- 1/4 cup heavy cream
- 1/2 teaspoon vanilla extract
- Pinch of salt

Instructions:

For the Donuts:

> Preheat your oven to 350°F (175°C). Grease a donut pan.
> In a large bowl, whisk together the flour, sugar, baking powder, baking soda, and salt.
> In another bowl, mix together the buttermilk, cooled brewed coffee, vegetable oil, egg, and vanilla extract.
> Add the wet ingredients to the dry ingredients and stir until just combined. Do not overmix.
> Spoon the batter into a piping bag or a zip-top bag with the corner snipped off.
> Pipe the batter into the prepared donut pan, filling each cavity about 2/3 full.
> Bake for 10-12 minutes or until the donuts are firm and a toothpick inserted into the center comes out clean.

Allow the donuts to cool in the pan for a few minutes before transferring them to a wire rack to cool completely.

For the Caramel Glaze:

In a saucepan over medium heat, melt the butter.
Stir in the brown sugar and cook until it dissolves, stirring constantly.
Add the heavy cream, vanilla extract, and a pinch of salt. Bring the mixture to a simmer and cook for 2-3 minutes until the caramel thickens.
Remove the caramel from heat and let it cool slightly.

Assembly:

Dip the tops of each cooled donut into the caramel glaze, ensuring they are well coated.
Place the glazed donuts on a wire rack to allow excess glaze to drip off.
Allow the glaze to set for a few minutes before serving.
Enjoy your Caramel Macchiato Donuts with the rich and comforting flavors of caramel and coffee!

These donuts capture the essence of a classic caramel macchiato, making them a perfect choice for a special breakfast or a delightful dessert. The caramel glaze adds a sweet and luscious finish to these coffee-infused treats.

Rosemary Olive Oil Donuts

Ingredients:

For the Donuts:

- 1 1/2 cups all-purpose flour
- 1/2 cup granulated sugar
- 1 1/2 teaspoons baking powder
- 1/4 teaspoon baking soda
- 1/4 teaspoon salt
- 1/2 cup buttermilk
- 1/4 cup extra virgin olive oil
- 1 large egg
- 1 teaspoon vanilla extract
- 1 tablespoon fresh rosemary, finely chopped

For the Glaze:

- 1 cup powdered sugar
- 2 tablespoons extra virgin olive oil
- 1-2 tablespoons milk (adjust for desired consistency)
- Additional chopped fresh rosemary for garnish (optional)

Instructions:

For the Donuts:

Preheat your oven to 350°F (175°C). Grease a donut pan.
In a large bowl, whisk together the flour, sugar, baking powder, baking soda, and salt.
In another bowl, mix together the buttermilk, olive oil, egg, vanilla extract, and chopped rosemary.
Add the wet ingredients to the dry ingredients and stir until just combined. Do not overmix.
Spoon the batter into a piping bag or a zip-top bag with the corner snipped off.
Pipe the batter into the prepared donut pan, filling each cavity about 2/3 full.

Bake for 10-12 minutes or until the donuts are firm and a toothpick inserted into the center comes out clean.

Allow the donuts to cool in the pan for a few minutes before transferring them to a wire rack to cool completely.

For the Glaze:

In a bowl, whisk together the powdered sugar, olive oil, and milk until smooth.

Assembly:

Dip the tops of each cooled donut into the olive oil glaze, ensuring they are well coated.

Place the glazed donuts on a wire rack to allow excess glaze to drip off.

Optionally, sprinkle additional chopped fresh rosemary on top for a savory touch.

Allow the glaze to set for a few minutes before serving.

Enjoy your Rosemary Olive Oil Donuts with the delightful combination of savory rosemary and rich olive oil!

These donuts offer a unique and sophisticated flavor profile, making them a perfect choice for a special breakfast or a delightful snack. The addition of olive oil provides a rich and moist texture, while the rosemary adds a fragrant and savory element.

Banana Foster Donuts

Ingredients:

For the Donuts:

- 1 1/2 cups all-purpose flour
- 1/2 cup brown sugar, packed
- 1 1/2 teaspoons baking powder
- 1/4 teaspoon baking soda
- 1/4 teaspoon salt
- 1/2 cup buttermilk
- 1/4 cup unsalted butter, melted
- 1 large egg
- 1 teaspoon vanilla extract
- 1 ripe banana, mashed

For the Banana Foster Glaze:

- 1/2 cup unsalted butter
- 1 cup brown sugar, packed
- 1/4 cup dark rum
- 1/4 cup banana liqueur (or banana-flavored syrup)
- Pinch of cinnamon (optional)

Instructions:

For the Donuts:

Preheat your oven to 350°F (175°C). Grease a donut pan.
In a large bowl, whisk together the flour, brown sugar, baking powder, baking soda, and salt.
In another bowl, mix together the buttermilk, melted butter, egg, vanilla extract, and mashed banana.
Add the wet ingredients to the dry ingredients and stir until just combined. Do not overmix.

Spoon the batter into a piping bag or a zip-top bag with the corner snipped off.
Pipe the batter into the prepared donut pan, filling each cavity about 2/3 full.
Bake for 10-12 minutes or until the donuts are firm and a toothpick inserted into the center comes out clean.
Allow the donuts to cool in the pan for a few minutes before transferring them to a wire rack to cool completely.

For the Banana Foster Glaze:

In a saucepan over medium heat, melt the butter.
Stir in the brown sugar, dark rum, banana liqueur (or banana-flavored syrup), and a pinch of cinnamon if desired.
Cook the mixture, stirring constantly, until it thickens into a glossy glaze (about 5-7 minutes).

Assembly:

Dip the tops of each cooled donut into the warm Banana Foster glaze, ensuring they are well coated.
Place the glazed donuts on a wire rack to allow excess glaze to drip off.
Allow the glaze to set for a few minutes before serving.
Enjoy your Banana Foster Donuts with the rich and decadent flavors of banana, brown sugar, and rum!

These donuts capture the essence of the classic Banana Foster dessert, making them a perfect choice for a special breakfast or a delightful dessert. The warm and boozy glaze adds an extra layer of indulgence to these delicious treats.

Chocolate Hazel Crunch Donuts

Ingredients:

For the Donuts:

- 1 1/2 cups all-purpose flour
- 1/2 cup granulated sugar
- 1/4 cup unsweetened cocoa powder
- 1 1/2 teaspoons baking powder
- 1/4 teaspoon baking soda
- 1/4 teaspoon salt
- 1/2 cup buttermilk
- 1/4 cup vegetable oil
- 1 large egg
- 1 teaspoon vanilla extract
- 1/4 cup hazelnuts, finely chopped

For the Chocolate Hazelnut Glaze:

- 1/2 cup chocolate hazelnut spread (like Nutella)
- 1 cup powdered sugar
- 2-3 tablespoons milk

For the Hazelnut Crunch Topping:

- 1/2 cup hazelnuts, finely chopped and toasted
- 2 tablespoons granulated sugar
- Pinch of salt

Instructions:

For the Donuts:

Preheat your oven to 350°F (175°C). Grease a donut pan.
In a large bowl, whisk together the flour, sugar, cocoa powder, baking powder, baking soda, and salt.
In another bowl, mix together the buttermilk, vegetable oil, egg, and vanilla extract.

Add the wet ingredients to the dry ingredients and stir until just combined. Do not overmix.

Fold in the finely chopped hazelnuts.

Spoon the batter into a piping bag or a zip-top bag with the corner snipped off.

Pipe the batter into the prepared donut pan, filling each cavity about 2/3 full.

Bake for 10-12 minutes or until the donuts are firm and a toothpick inserted into the center comes out clean.

Allow the donuts to cool in the pan for a few minutes before transferring them to a wire rack to cool completely.

For the Chocolate Hazelnut Glaze:

In a bowl, whisk together the chocolate hazelnut spread, powdered sugar, and milk until smooth.

For the Hazelnut Crunch Topping:

In a small bowl, mix together the finely chopped and toasted hazelnuts, granulated sugar, and a pinch of salt.

Assembly:

Dip the tops of each cooled donut into the chocolate hazelnut glaze, ensuring they are well coated.

Immediately sprinkle the hazelnut crunch topping on the glazed donuts.

Place the glazed and topped donuts on a wire rack to allow excess glaze to drip off.

Allow the glaze to set for a few minutes before serving.

Enjoy your Chocolate Hazelnut Crunch Donuts with the perfect combination of rich chocolate, hazelnuts, and a delightful crunch!

These donuts offer a decadent and nutty flavor profile, making them a perfect choice for a special breakfast or a delightful dessert. The hazelnut crunch topping adds an extra layer of texture and indulgence to these delicious treats.

www.ingramcontent.com/pod-product-compliance
Lightning Source LLC
LaVergne TN
LVHW081553060526
838201LV00054B/1883